DATE DUE

How to Live with Your Computer

PAUL T. SMITH

How to Live
With Your Computer

A Nontechnical Guide for Managers

AMERICAN MANAGEMENT ASSOCIATION

To my dearest critic and helper—Marjorie

Preface

Experience in the use of data processing equipment has been gained by trial and error. Whether this method of learning is right or wrong—and it has been a blend of both—management has viewed it with tolerant understanding.

Here are fabulous opportunities to increase earnings. The manager, properly supported by intelligently applied systems, may look at the "big picture" or go straight to the heart of a problem area. With today's high cost, however, tolerant understanding is no longer acceptable or sufficient, if ever it was, for developing a sensible approach to mechanized business systems. Experience measured only by time will also be found wanting.

An official of a corporation noted for its inefficient use of data processing machines and systems has described its programs as a means of gaining management experience. One does not question the sincerity of this statement, nor can it be denied that experience does accrue and so appear to justify the necessary "stretching" that such a definition implies. But, however justifiable it may seem now, tolerance may deteriorate into a semblance of apathy as more complicated and efficient machines, still inexpertly used, lead to chaos.

Another executive has said: "After six years of heavy investment in computers, I cannot say they are helping me personally to do a better job."[1] This statement is echoed by many.

What brought on such a condition? One reason is that top management people have been obliged to keep their noses to other grindstones. Deploring the "papermill" and its costs, they have hoped the computer would be the tool they needed to deal with it. And indeed, during this decade of tremendous industrial growth, computer technology and capacity have kept pace with the need. A hundred new models of computers were announced between 1955 and 1964; only

[1] John T. Garrity, "The Management Information Dream: The End or a New Beginning," *Financial Executive*, September 1964.

7

a tenth of that number had appeared on the market before 1955. Management had no time, however, to study their uses and what it wanted from them; often equipment was ordered in desperation. The use of the machines was left to the discretion of operating people, frequently at low levels, and the program was usually devoid of management policy direction. In too many companies, these are still standard practices. Why is this so? In some cases it is because fear of unfamiliar, complex, and costly equipment, added to poor communication with the technicians who are familiar with it, are allowed to become major deterrents to rigorous management action. *Effective results will come only when management is adequately informed.*

Clarence B. Randall has said that everyone writes about business except businessmen. Therefore, while many business books titillate the businessman reader and offer him general educational value, they supply few practical solutions to real-life business problems. In contrast, we have directed our efforts in the present volume toward only the most pertinent points, commenting frankly on the management problems in data processing and proposing workable solutions to them.

We may sometimes seem critical of management. If so, it is not from lack of respect but merely for the purpose of suggesting areas where improvement is in order. Some of our comments, too, may arouse the ire of the equipment manufacturer. However, on sober reflection he will recognize that the future of his business depends on good management practice in the use of his products.

Much of the book's space has been given over to a discussion of business systems. A system is described as "a whole composed of parts in orderly arrangement according to some scheme or plan." To manage is "to control the course of affairs by one's own actions." It follows that the act of managing must include control of the course of affairs by developing the scheme or plan by which the various parts may become the whole—in this case, the business system. Conclusion: Systems and managerial responsibilities are inseparable.

Management is on the threshold of a new era; the next decade will add luster to an already glamorous field. However, this new era will also bring with it an exponential increase in the complexity of management problems. We will discover that the alluring, beautifully designed data processing equipment of the future, again improperly managed, will only compound our problems of the past ten years. In fact—regardless of the equipment used, now or in the future —management problems will be the same, and they are the timeless fabric of this book.

It is the sole purpose of these pages to offer management, with much truth if little eloquence, beneficial counsel in the use of a marvelous tool. The material here recorded reflects actual experiences, good and bad, with observations on the reasons for both success and failure. May the reader find in it ideas which will help to enhance the benefits of mechanization and increase company earnings—and may life in general be a little bit easier because of it.

Writing about the management aspects of data processing has been a difficult job, for they are indeed complex and difficult to put on paper. It has been an easier task, however, because of the tireless efforts of the wonderfully talented editorial staff of the American Management Association.

Over the years I have been blessed by the good counsel and inspiration of many; in the area of general management, men like George R. Bynum, Curtis H. Cadenhead, H. L. Howard, and Robert McCulloch have given kind attention to my needs for guidance and help. In the fields of business systems and data processing I am especially appreciative of the valuable association with such talented men as Charles L. Davis, J. M. Mayes, Richard G. Pfeiffer, and O. F. Waldeck. My sincerest thanks to these men and to others unlisted but still remembered.

PAUL T. SMITH

Contents

PART ONE:

Data Processing—A Management View

If we reflect on the history and development of data processing equipment, we will see the computer as an amalgamation and expansion of the capabilities of many commonplace office machines that more than ever require knowledgeable direction by man.

1. Defining the Subject

Machine technology has far outreached man's ability to use this new capability. During the past quarter of a century, all the major data processing machine developments have come about—and yet, in the same period, management understanding of their uses, at least in a collective sense, has increased very little. This is the fundamental reason for the many failures and disappointing fiscal results.

Management has been busy with other important and trying tasks, not the least of which is expansion of facilities to satisfy burgeoning markets—in short, not enough time has been available to cope with the problem. Now the need to focus attention on the computer has become critical, and many executives are fearful that it may already be too late. But we should not despair—there is still time to begin a well-planned counterattack.

Weary, red-eyed readers can attest to the fact that millions of words have been written about "using" data processing equipment. Here, instead, we are interested in how to "manage" the function. Here we will sort out the important management considerations from the confusing mass of technical gobbledegook.

Before getting fully into the subject, let us define the equipment. A computer, or electronic data processing machine (EDPM), is a data processor; surprisingly, so is a typewriter. Strictly defined, all office machinery must be classified as data processing equipment: cash registers, adding machines, calculators, Comptometers, posting machines, keypunch machines, multipliers, interpreters, printers. The computer is capable of processing information electronically from punched cards or magnetic tape. Computers are slow-speed and high-speed, large and small. Their prices vary according to capability, speed, and competitive pressures.

We are concerned not with models or makes of machines but with the problems of managing an identifiable group of data processing equipment beyond the ledger posting machine—that is, from punched card processors, or electric accounting machines (EAM), through programed computers (EDPM). We shall avoid detailed descriptions of the mechanics of these machines; rather, in harmony with our purpose, we shall take a management view of their uses.

Early Punched Card Equipment

Not many years ago a new machine, the punched card sorter, was demonstrated. The salesman placed cards of various colors in the hopper and proudly announced his intention to sort them into different pockets.

Obviously, we thought, the man was deranged; the colors were thoroughly mixed. To our amazement, however, he did indeed sort them perfectly. He stood at smiling attention while we applauded the feat, viewing it as if it were witchcraft, with a mixture of awe and distrust. Then, after holding us in suspense for a time, he told us the secret: The colors were coded by holes punched in the cards— No. 1 was white, No. 2 was blue, and so on. What trickery! But, still, the function was of little use as far as we could see. Who cared about sorting colors?

With monumental patience the salesman described how the holes could be punched in a card, how this could be arranged with other punched cards for sorting in any order desired, and how the punched information could even be printed on another machine called a "tabulator." Not only could data be printed, but specific groups could be totaled in the process. Cards could be tabulated (summarized), or they could be "listed" to show the detail which made up the totals. One tabulator model could perform "direct subtraction" while another cheaper one subtracted by adding complement input. For example, to subtract 123 from 1,020, add the complement of 123 and drop the 9's at the left of the answer:

$$
\begin{array}{r}
1\ 020 \\
9\ 877 \\
\hline
90\ 897
\end{array}
$$

Neither model could print alphabetic information or even very much numeric.

Once we adjusted to this new way of thinking and considered the possibilities of such equipment in solving business problems, acceptance was assured. This was early punched card accounting. Now we refer to punched card machines as EAM and to computers as EDPM.

Differences Between EAM and EDPM

The term "EAM" (electric accounting machines) may seem to be a misnomer, since the machines were used for purposes other than accounting. Not that the name is important; but, when we evaluate the equipment's capability, we should not apply the definition in its strict professional sense. As a punched card is processed through EAM equipment, it becomes a tool for measuring or establishing responsibility and accountability, whether or not it has specific application to fiscal activity.

The internal capability of EAM equipment is circumscribed; it has little room for the logical processes the programed computer performs so speedily and effortlessly. EAM equipment must be instructed within the limits of its external brain—the plugboard. As a generalization we might say that the plugboard, when properly wired, will persuade the machine—that is, the intelligence which is built into the internal works—to do the tricks it has "learned."

The term "EDPM" (electronic data processing machines) describes another, more dramatic group of machines with an almost limitless capability to perform computation processes. Man's intellect has been supplemented, even expanded, by what we have come to call a "mechanical" or "electronic" brain. This is not appropriate terminology, however, and—although convenient—it is lazy thinking to accept such an oversimplification as an accurate description. The machine is not itself a brain; it is an untiring plagiarist, operating only on the logic fed to it by its instructor. It is a repetitious imbecile but—most of the time—an accurate, obedient one. Once given its chores, it can mimic the instructor over and over at fantastic speeds.

Therefore, the computer is different from EAM equipment in one major respect: It has the ability to perform its tricks internally. We can instruct it in this way: Multiply A times B, then add the sum (C) to D; compare D to X, which is in a predetermined memory address, and select the lesser of the two amounts (D or X) to add to Y.

This is an overly simplified description of a computer routine, as it is intended to be. The important thing is to recognize the relationship between the machine's actions and our own thought processes. The machine "thinks" much as we do—that is, its actions parallel and work in concert with our thoughts—because our thoughts determine what it does. Before we ask a computer to do anything, we must "program" or think it out first. The salient point is that we have to think the problem through only once. Then the computer performs the operation over and over as long as we desire.

Automatic Data Processing

The term "automatic data processing" was not a credible description of a procedure until a few years ago. Compare, for example, the handling of a payroll check by EAM in the 1940's and by EDPM in the 1960's. The logic of the EAM procedure was simply to perform a specific task and give an answer. If payroll deductions exceeded gross pay, the answer came out negative. Without proper controls, the old multiplier might therefore cause a paycheck to be written for the negative result. Thus:

Gross pay	$100.00
Deductions	102.00
Net pay	$998.00 (complement)

Although obviously this is wrong, the error was difficult to find unless the operator used some human logic in system design.

Since it was possible for a one-week paycheck to have five digits but not six, the card could be designed with a six-digit net pay field (group of card columns). If this was done, the machine handled the problem this way:

Gross pay	$0100.00
Deductions	0102.00
Net pay	$9998.00 (complement)

This method allowed the operator to check for the presence of zeros in the sixth position (thousands) and remove the credit net earnings (nines in the sixth place). A minimum could then be set and a new card could be made with deductions selected in order of preference until net pay equaled $5.00 or whatever was established as the minimum. Controls had to be changed manually to keep a control total balance on deductions. This was a laborious procedure, of course, and it certainly was not "automatic."

The computer really does approach the problem automatically. For example:

Gross pay	$100.00
Deductions:	
Federal tax (computed)	10.00
Preference 1	50.00 leaves $40.00
Preference 2	42.00 leaves −2.00
Drop preference 2	− leaves 40.00
Total deductions	60.00
Net pay	$40.00

The computer may be programed to carry a list of "unused" deductions for balancing purposes. This may be an "output" on cards or tape, or it may be printed out at the console. The logic may also be set up to make deductions to the point of minimum earnings (say, $5.00), so that $35.00 of the third deduction can also be made.

Here is a paradox which the alert reader may have already discovered. Men wearing green eye shades and garters on their sleeves could have performed this operation automatically in the same manner as the computer; the "new" EAM equipment of the time seemed to take us backward. This is a truism of a sort. The old EAM equipment had little logic; but it did have speed for its day, and when it made errors it did so consistently. This allowed for anticipation of logic error and for system design to correct the mistakes (exceptions) as in our simple example. The technician was therefore able to develop his own methods to correct faulty machine logic. He may, for instance, have designed his own "routine" to be performed in a separate machine operation to correct the errors of a previous run. Automatic data processing machines now do this simultaneously in the same run. (See the accompanying exhibit.)

A Brief History

It is doubtful that World War II could have been successfully terminated so early without EAM equipment. Huge plants employed tens of thousands of workers who were paid every week. The preparation of payrolls for these plants, the accumulation of contract costs, and other tremendous administrative and logistic tasks were assigned to the "tabulating" organization. This period provided the first great proving ground for data processing. It also established the need for better machines with improved logic and speed.

While EAM equipment ground laboriously on with its task of helping the business world, the computer was also doing its part in the war effort, literally coming into its own along with the atomic bomb. Whether the bomb or the computer has made the greatest impact on civilization will remain a moot question for some time to come.

The computer appeared on the business scene as a scientific calculator, and we were content to keep it that way for quite some time. It is difficult to determine whether blame for its slow development should be laid at a specific doorstep or whether it simply required the evolutionary period for human beings to comprehend it. The latter may be true, however—for, with all its latent possibilities, the computer marked time while human imagination caught up.

If any one technical problem was a major barrier during the formative stages, it was input-output capability. (Input is information to be processed; output is processed or printed information.) The first computer actively marketed was a card-operated machine, shamefully slow at input, equally laggard at computing, and inept at putting out information. Expanded use of the card-operated computer brought more demands for increased input-output speed, and shortly thereafter tremendous strides were made in developing the next generation; this was the first business computer to use cards and magnetic tape. The close proximity of the card-programed computer to the next development leads one to believe that this computer was intended strictly as a training machine to test the water and that it was marketed—quite wisely—to generate enthusiasm about the idea of computing. It caught on quite well among scientific people, and the solving of engineering problems on such equipment became

MACHINE LOGIC DIAGRAM—PAYROLL DEDUCTIONS

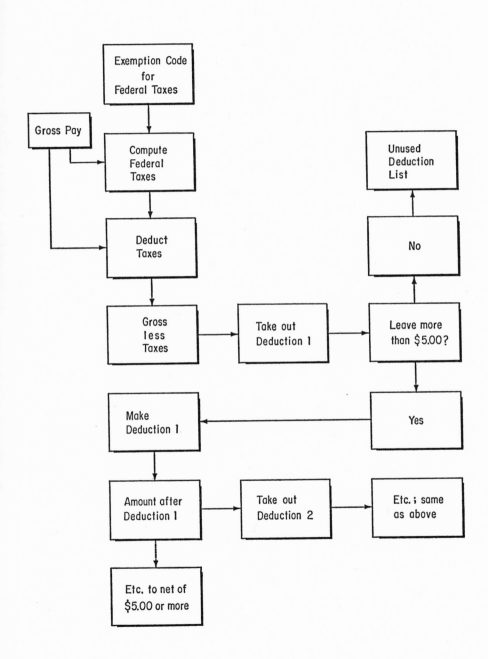

commonplace. It is difficult, however, to determine if the stir of scientific imagination hastened the development of the equipment or if the reverse was true.

There was a lull of two or three years between the appearance of the card-programed calculator and management's grudging acquiescence to the use of computers in dealing with business problems. Slowly, very slowly, the business world accepted the idea of automatic data processing. Helping to overcome the suspicion and distrust was the patient manufacturer, who offered the equipment in configurations the mind could gradually comprehend and accept. There is little doubt that some interim steps in this educational process could have been dropped, but acceptance would certainly have been slower because of lack of comprehension.

People and the Computer

Automatic data processing may best be defined as an organized way of thinking—not simply a machine process but an application of human knowledge within the bounds of machine capability. The modern computer has built-in logic capabilities which are almost unlimited in flexibility. Therefore, the performance of machine routines is dependent primarily on what the systems man and technician ask of the equipment. The payoff to the user is in direct ratio to the amount of human knowledge put into the system and its introduction into the computer. This point deserves much thought. For instance, a factory superintendent would not dream of putting a neophyte in charge of an expensive and complicated milling machine. He would certainly select the most experienced and capable man available, though he might wisely put the beginner there to study under him. The reasons for this are obvious, yet many managers who buy expensive and complicated computers give little thought to the capabilities they should require in their systems men: They consider the mere decision to acquire a computer as a harbinger of happy and profitable days ahead.

Often heard is the statement, "The computer does this," or, "The computer made that mistake." Data processing equipment, like a milling machine, is inanimate. It will perform only as instructed; it can take no responsibility for its actions, good or bad. Like any other facility, the computer is no more efficient than the person responsible for it.

Management's information needs are not altered by the presence of the computer; the machine merely offers a means of providing information faster and more economically.

2. Data Processing—
A Way of Thinking

WE HAVE DESCRIBED AUTOMATIC DATA PROCESSING AS AN ORGANIZED way of thinking; now the word "automatic" will be dropped. The term is fanciful because the connotation is that the machine does the job automatically. But in fact the machine's only truly automatic action is its repetition of operating instructions; man must specify the act of logic the machine is to perform. Man's knowledge therefore becomes the fountainhead of any data processing system—a claim which deserves further examination.

Any business system has, or should have, as its purpose the improvement or surveillance of some phase of the business. That is, it is designed to gather usable data which will facilitate that improvement or surveillance and to hold someone accountable for results which the data will portray. If the system utilizes hand methods, we find ourselves evaluating its human elements: Which man can best supervise the job? Which clerk is most accurate? If we introduce machines, we think in terms of equipment and its capabilities: Which computer will best suit our needs and give us sufficient, though not excessive, capacity?

Whether we do the job by hand or by machine, however, we have to consider responsibility for system input at some level of preparation. This is normally a manual function; where data are machine-processed, it will be a duty assigned outside the computer center.

At the machine processing level, ability to perform is necessarily evaluated in terms of equipment capability; evaluation of people, on their ability to generate maximum performance from the machine. Clearly, therefore, since human dexterity is still required, data processing equipment is most certainly a means of achieving an end and not an end in itself. Also, machines cannot react to assignment of responsibility. Only people can do this.

Responsibility and Accountability

When we reflect on assignment of responsibility, we may well conclude that accountability is enhanced by the very act of assigning responsibility. As a matter of fact, the need for accountability sired the creation of management to define boundaries within which responsibility could be assigned and evaluated. Thus it is axiomatic that responsibility and accountability must go hand in hand to accomplish the desired management act of promoting and measuring operations, with or without the computer.

In all human endeavor, data processing not excepted, the problem of overindulgence shows its ugly self. We often speak of the tools of management; but when we look closely at the manager standing before his "work bench" surrounded by the tools of his trade, we sometimes question whether he has become expert with any of them. He seems to be in a state of confusion as to which tool he should use. An oversupply of equipment and insufficient study of business requirements have too often led him to select a machine when a pencil would have done the job. So it is with the computer—many managers expect it will prove a panacea for all business ills.

Since the advent of the computer, accountability has often been allowed to erode into a vulgar display of voluminous reports conceived in frenzy and perpetuated in pride. Expansive, incomprehensible reports suggest the presence of responsibility in areas incapable of reacting or demonstrating any semblance of accountability. This lack of response is then appraised as indicating a need for myriad other reports in even more remote areas. So spreads the ripple in the report pond.

Example: A large electronics firm decided a computer would be the solution to its problems in manufacturing control. Little consideration was given to business needs and the "real world" problems related to the manufacturing control processes. Instead, a machine was secured for the singular purpose of "putting manufacturing control on a high-speed computer." The system was hastily conceived—without being put in writing—then described in vague terms to a group of programers who set about the task of "using the computer." Result:

A weekly report with eight copies, one of which stood 11 feet high! This report was, of course, prepared on a high-speed printer; in fact, the biggest problem in using it was that it took longer to remove the carbon than to do the printing. Sometimes this step was not finished before the next report was published. Worst of all, the fundamental considerations—the subtle refinements which make a good business system—were forgotten. The company had mountains of data but little management information. The marked decline in profits that followed was directly attributable to misuse of data processing equipment.

In another case, a manufacturing firm was faced with the need for cost control. Its system was "designed" by technicians without any management participation. The result was a monthly cost report requiring 250 boxes of expensive forms. Indeed, the paper cost more than the printing cost on the high-speed printer. Moreover, one month's supply of paper for use in the report outweighed a month's output of the company's product. Ridiculous, but true.

As these cases point up, data processing equipment is very often used to create detail instead of being put to its intended uses. The machines can take large quantities of disorganized data and arrange them in summary form for a bifocal review by management. Yet, because it has been so generally misused, some people now assess the computer as merely a means of providing large amounts of detail to a host of confused users.

The High-Speed Printer—Enemy of Good Systems Design

The high-speed printer can operate at the rate of 1,200 lines a minute or even more, with each line made up of 100-plus characters of "information." There may be occasions when voluminous output is required, but how many times do we hear: "Print it all. It will only take ten minutes!" Twelve thousand lines, more characters than in a lengthy novel—and all in just ten minutes!

The high-speed printer, in short, is a management tool that requires much control. Its very speed, however desirable in theory, offers a convenient excuse for avoiding the responsibilities of good system design; it becomes a crutch to the systems man whose decision to "print it all" forces the manager to struggle through the haystack of paper to locate the needle of information he requires. And why is this? Most often it is because of the complete lack of communication between the user (management) and the supplier (the computer organization).

Machine Effect on Management Desire for Information

We will find on close analysis that the equipment being used, if any, has little influence on management's basic desires or requirements for information. This is one of the reasons why data processing is a way of thinking. The manager who must rely on hand methods of gathering information must tailor his requirements to fit the ability of his people and the time available. If he can take advantage of data processing equipment, he can adjust his needs upward to match the machine's capability. In both cases, however, his requirements can be the same.

The use of hand methods necessarily calls for considerable thought on the part of the manager, limited as he is by definable human boundaries. Since he may so greatly expand his desires where he has access to equipment, he may therefore become careless about curbing quantity requirements and setting quality standards. Even though comparable levels of efficiency may be achieved by hand and by machine, the volume of data and paper created by inefficient use of the machine system will add a confusion factor at an exponential rate, usually in proportion to the number of "users."

Systems evaluation in its proper perspective might best be represented by a pyramid whose crest is the end product of information needed by management. Unlike the physical pyramid, it must be built from the top down. By defining the major points of accountability, management establishes the angles at which the sides extend toward the base on which the system will stand. This is the secret of bifocal vision in management systems.

The personal time managers give to establishing business needs for information will serve to match the price with the product.

3. Business Needs

Exploring one specific technical area of data processing would be much easier than covering the entire subject. But management's needs and problems vary widely, as do the tools available to meet the needs: One manager may be satisfied with present uses of his equipment; others may now have equipment which they want to update or improve; and still others, bless their backward ways, may not use data processing equipment at all. Further complicating any attempt at full coverage is the diversity of application. If we were to give attention to all the variables these and other differences generate in determining the need for and the use of equipment, we could explode this discussion to the point of infinite verbosity.

The basic motive behind the decision to begin, or continue, to use data processing equipment should not be different from that which determines the acquisition or retention of a building. Need must be established on the basis of sensible criteria which may be summed up in one question: Does it, or will it, make money for us? There are those who will claim that even though the installation of data processing equipment does not save dollars, it makes more information available to management and, for that reason alone, should be installed.

Information is important to management. Statistics not otherwise available may be produced with data processing equipment and, if truly useful, become a factor in income production. Though such statistics may be intangible and impossible of dollar evaluation, management may wisely consider it worthwhile to produce them. In making a decision of this kind, however, we must beware of the dangers of the "creep."

The "creep" is a repetitive report which is conceived in a crisis, promptly forgotten when the crisis is passed, but still produced on a regular schedule. When the necessity for such a report is questioned, the answer may sound like this: "Mr. Barnes started it in 1959 to determine whether age grouping and color of eyes among salesmen have any correlation with dollars of sales in the different areas." Mr. Barnes left the company two years ago.

Case history No. 1: A company consulted an expert in data processing about its need for more computer equipment. A study of the company's systems and information needs revealed not only that no new data processing equipment should be installed but that the existing equipment was unnecessary and its use should be discontinued.

Most data processing manufacturers do not want to rent or sell their equipment to companies that cannot profitably use it; to do so will eventually give them a bad name. But times and circumstances change; in the case just cited, the company's business had changed, and so had its information needs. As a result, even its equipment had become a creep.

Case history No. 2: A firm was faced with the necessity of ordering additional equipment because of the heavy demands on its machines. A survey was made of its computer workload, including an audit of report usage. The result was that 20 per cent of the reports were discontinued—they were creeps and, without the audit review, would have gone on costing the company a considerable amount of money to sustain them.

Case history No. 3: A data processing manager was certain that many of the reports he turned out were not actually used. To test his belief, he held those in question until they were called for by supposed users. Result: 18 reports were reduced to 8; some were eliminated, others were rearranged and consolidated, and the real need for information was served at considerably lower cost.

The Preliminary Survey

How can we determine whether data processing equipment is really needed? Although this question cannot be answered by listing a set of rules or by proposing a mathematical formula, there is one rule which will apply in every case. That is, before deciding to order, update, or retain equipment, we should first determine what the needs of the business really are—what it requires to grow and prosper. This question of business need must be answered before any other.

Once it is settled, the next questions may be posed: Must we have equipment to satisfy the needs of the business? If so, what kind? Obviously, these queries have no ready answers; but if we decide to look further at possible use only after determining actual needs, we will eventually arrive at the correct answers. The accompanying exhibit illustrates the route management follows in determining its need for a data processing study.

Let us look into the systems required to meet business needs. Systems design is the important consideration here. Most of us ought to redesign our systems, whether we recognize it or not, and if we use data processing equipment without pondering this fundamental facet of a solid information program, we are spending too much money.

An excellent way to survey the need for data processing equipment —or, as a variation, to evaluate the present information program— is to have every manager in the company give some "honest" time to compiling a list of the most pressing operating problems of the business. After proper brainstorming, group the problems into like items. To make this an effective method, we must be sure that each manager understands the importance of his participation and what the decision may eventually mean to him.

Likely to be prominent on the managers' lists are lack of information, peak loads, and great quantities of detail. These are, of course, promising areas for exploration. Often, however, though these problems appear so adaptable to machine methods, they can be solved by other, less costly means. Distasteful as it may be to the proponent of data processing machine usage, management may decide, upon review of the lists, to cease processing some of the detail or to short-cut relatively unimportant procedures which have crept into what started out as a simple system. A rearranged schedule can often reduce peak loads to the extent that they are no longer troublesome, with or without equipment. Further, we may find that many listed items do not qualify as business needs.

At this point the decision we must make is this: Is our potential for machine data processing still sufficiently promising and adaptable to warrant further study? One way to find out (for those who do not now use computers, particularly) is to select the most complicated of the existing problems and make a rough determination of the number of input records, then ask the nearest data processing service

MANAGEMENT LOGIC TRAIL
TO DETERMINE NEED FOR DATA PROCESSING STUDY

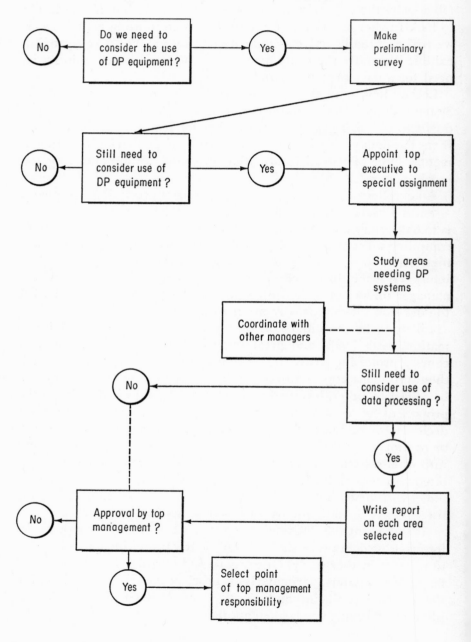

bureau to estimate separately the cost of preparing the machine input and of running one report from these data. At this juncture, approximations are sufficient, so if three reports are needed in different sequences from the same data, trebling the printing cost of one report is good enough. Preliminary though they may be, the calculations may be eye-openers.

To supplement these estimates, we need others which we can make ourselves. For example: How much does it cost to do the jobs by hand? We should be able to answer this easily. If we convert to a machine system, how much would it cost to keypunch or otherwise prepare manual input—the source documents—for machine language? This question, too, should be easily answered.

These rough figures may show savings, but will the savings be large enough to absorb the costs of rental or amortization of our own equipment—plus operators, supervision, supplies, and facility costs? If it looks promising to this point, the preliminary study may be broadened to include other qualifying jobs. Similar calculations should be made for them, and they can then be added to the trial job or jobs. After this is done, we are ready for the test of basic cost recovery.

Now to a reputable equipment manufacturer (two might be better). What equipment will best do the jobs selected in the study? What machine does the manufacturer advise? How much will it cost to rent or buy and to operate? Who has similar equipment in actual use?

Should his information and experience show that no savings against basic costs will result from a change to computer operation, the reputable manufacturer will so advise you. If there are no additional jobs to be added to the present workload and the computer people cannot show how to produce savings by converting the existing jobs to machine operation, you will be no more successful. If, however, the manufacturer does tell you that you will save money by using his machines, get a summation of his study in writing; then visit a user of the same equipment and verify the calculations. Such a step should be taken, not because you mistrust the manufacturer, but because it is good business practice to confirm his findings; further, you may have forgotten something that will come to mind when you talk to another equipment user. You should therefore question him carefully about all phases of the operation including machine reliability and maintenance service, with particular emphasis on the latter.

Let us assume that all the answers are affirmative—that a real need for acquiring or retaining data processing equipment is indicated. If so, it is time to re-evaluate the important systems aspects of the problem. Are the systems now in use both capable and intelligent? Do they produce too little or too much? Systems should be reviewed very carefully; we may discover that some operations which previously passed muster are now unnecessary. Moreover, the very process of review may force us to take a completely new look at previous affirmations of the need for data processing equipment. This is an important point, and attention to it will pay in direct ratio to management effort.

We should not be too concerned for the moment with the question whether or not our existing systems may be transferred "as is" to the machines—we can be sure they cannot. Our real interest is, are they currently satisfying our needs? If so, we are comparing apples and apples; that is, satisfactory performance with manual or present equipment and satisfactory performance with new equipment, if the intelligent utilization of new machines is still possible.

The present user of equipment may question the application of such a procedure to the evaluation of his machine operations. If he does, he may prefer to approach an evaluation of his systems from a different route; for instance, he can simply pick one job as performed at present and request a service bureau to make an estimate on it so that its relative efficiency can be compared. The bureau's evaluation should provide a rough basis for deciding whether the remaining jobs are worth studying and whether, in fact, a full survey might be in order.

The systems purist will no doubt disagree violently with such bungling methods in reaching the decision to survey the need for equipment. Even though only a preliminary study is at stake, he can argue that subsequent changes in systems and procedures, made at the formal-study level, will add or detract from the values used in making the rough determination of need. He will be right, of course—but, at the same time, how many managers can afford to wait for a "total system" study before considering the need for a data processing program?

Case history: A large aircraft company which was a big user of data processing equipment decided to set up a systems research group to develop the total systems approach to all its business needs. Two years and $200,000 later, the total system was not totaled. There were beautiful brochures, some in color, and a wall 60 feet long was draped with all the forms in present use. Codes had been developed to describe need, action, routing, responsibility, and much more. But no one understood all this except the total systems man, if indeed he did himself. When the program's accomplishments were evaluated, it was found that, given another two years and another $200,000, the company would still be using the same expensive equipment in the same inefficient manner. The program was stopped, and the group was disbanded. Quite a different approach showed results in six months.

Need for Conservatism

Most cases call for a decision within a more reasonable time limit than two years. We should do well, however, to pay some attention to the purist—at least to his exhortation in support of conservatism.

As an analogy, consider the hauler in need of a truck. He is in the business of transporting gravel and must take into consideration the economics of purchasing new equipment. His decision he will make by answering one question: Will it make money for me? This he will determine by estimating the number and size of loads to forecast revenue levels. Only after the various levels of revenue are estimated should he attempt to decide which machine will produce optimum return. Then, even after making the decision based on gravel loads, he may well ask himself, "What else will I be likely to haul, and will this truck do the job?" Possibly the kinds and size of rock loads he anticipates hauling will affect his final decision, but he certainly will not consider hauling bulk oil in a gravel truck. For him this is not a business need; therefore, it will not be a factor in his decision.

Conservatism is desirable when making the decision to use or expand a data processing capability. For example, one company laid down a rule that estimated savings on new projects—that is, additions to the existing total program of data processing—would have to be five to one before installation would be allowed. This would have been a ridiculous limitation if it had been interpreted strictly, but it was not. Management, quite wisely, had decided that the five-to-one ratio would prevent excess optimism, knowing all the while that savings would in fact be closer to two to one in the final analysis —when the new project was installed.

How conservative a company must be in practice will, from a practical standpoint, depend on how critical the need is for accuracy. Some companies can allow little margin for error in their computations on computer-use savings; an error may cause bankruptcy—it has happened. Others, the large ones, may never know how close they come to their estimates. Laxity is not recommended, but it is practiced.

True, data processing machine applications can save considerable money, but we must avoid the common mistake of assuming that machines are always the answer to a problem. This simply is not so. Only thorough study by management will avoid the costs of such a misconception.

4. Decision and Organization

DECISIONS TO ENTER INTO A DATA PROCESSING PROGRAM ARE OFTEN made without benefit of adequate studies; sometimes they are even a result of emotional motivation. Perhaps management has been disturbed over dwindling earnings and has made the decision to install a computer simply because a successful competitor is using one. If such is the case, further deterioration of earnings may well be the result, not because of the equipment itself, but because the company is not ready to make profitable use of the systems advantages the equipment offers.

The Committee

Too often the task of investigating the possible use of equipment will be assigned at a point in the organization four or five levels below the top executive. Sometimes the ultimate point of reporting on such an assignment is a high management level, but usually the recommendations are evaluated by a committee appointed expressly for this purpose.

Although there may be notable exceptions, it must be said that the most consistent way to draw and quarter a data processing program is to set up such a committee. The reasons are quite simple, and they cast no aspersions on the character or ability of the committee members.

The most prominent characteristic of the committee member is his lack of time for such a project. He is preoccupied with the day-to-day duties of his line job. What he yearns for is immediate relief from current problems, and he finds it impossible to concentrate on a program which will theoretically solve his problems some time in the future. Moreover, he is bewildered by the variety of equipment and methods proposed for company use. He should not be expected to speak fluently about the machines and their capabilities; yet, even if his boss does not ask it of him, he may himself think it is necessary.

Nor can the committee member—being human and in charge of a specific function within the company—consider in an objective manner a proposal which will reduce his departmental manning by half. Regardless of how hard he may try to be objective, he cannot avoid examining each proposal in light of its effect on his own operation and on his own people. Though his loyalty to the company and his adherence to lofty principles are inviolate, he sees the threat to Joe's job; and Joe has a wife and three children to support. Thus filled with fear, apprehension, and varying degrees of distrust, the committee becomes entangled in its own reactions and moves every way but forward.

Committees are seldom effective in advancing data processing. A data processing system is in reality a cost reduction program, or it should be; but how often does a committee succeed in achieving cost reduction? Any sizable cost reduction is usually the result of top management mandate based on a less than scientific evaluation of cause and effect. There are, of course, better ways to bring about cost reductions and to make studies of data processing.

One-Man Decision

The minimum outlay for a small computer, including corollary costs, will range from $75,000 to $100,000 per year. Stated in terms of annual cost for occupying a building, this is the equivalent of 25,000 square feet of very good floor space. It is doubtful that any president would himself take complete responsibility for a decision about so large a capital expenditure without personal investigation. Yet such decisions are made every day on data processing—and at much lower levels in the organization. Many times, in fact, the task is left to a man who is several levels down but who in the opinion of his superiors possesses some mystic undefined power to make the correct decision. Automatic acquiescence in whatever he decides is not fair to the subordinate; he should not be required to assume so great a responsibility.

A Better Way

A better approach, and one more likely to succeed, is to have top management initiate the study after consideration of the broad survey discussed in the preceding chapter. Such a plan should include appointing a qualified middle- or top-management man, relieving him of other duties, and assigning him to study the problem. He should report at the highest possible level, even to the board of directors if conditions and dollars warrant it, and should be required to make regular reports, at least monthly. Each department head in the organization should be advised in writing as to the duties of the man assigned and should be directed to lend vigorous support to his task. Each should be asked to designate an official representative from his area to collaborate actively with him during the investigation. This kind of management support will get the program off the ground, but it is only the beginning.

Just as the eventual level of efficiency in a data processing program will be in direct ratio to the quality of this preliminary survey, so will the results of the preliminary study be in direct ratio to the ability and business acumen of the man assigned by top management. He must be perceptive to determine which are the bigger problems; he must also be possessed of practical logic to weigh time and money against the extent of the total problem. He will categorize jobs (systems) to be considered in this fashion:

Quick, with little payoff.
Quick, with big return.
Slow, with small savings.
Slow, with big return.

Easily installed jobs, even with small returns, are better than none, so if the data processing program is new to the company he will wisely decide that such jobs should be taken on immediately to produce some payoff. On the other hand, if the goal is one of updating and improving machine systems, he may decide to work on the difficult jobs with big potential first. These again are matters for judgment and not the subject of this book. Our purpose is to emphasize the necessity for selection of a qualified man to direct the investigation.

Documenting the Findings

Properly planned and manned, the study program should quickly take a definite direction. When areas of payoff are determined and presented for evaluation by management, a summary should be prepared on each proposed project covering at least the following:

- The specific problem, stated simply, briefly, and clearly.
- The answer—the way the problem can be solved with a data processing system.
- Schedule of time needed to design, program, and install the system.
- An adequate estimate of cost, including systems people, programers, operators, supplies, special facilities, and other related costs. These figures will allow computation of savings, after system installation, in terms of organization, and will indicate in advance whose toes will be trod upon.
- The cost of doubling up on the old system, running old and new parallel for a time. We may as well allow for adequate lap, since it happens every time. This and other R&D costs should be allocated over a reasonable payout period, lest showing the full amount in one early period mislead management. However, be careful to state that it has been amortized; accounting treatment may be different in that such costs may be written off the books immediately.
- Other advantages, such as more information, faster reporting, and ability to handle greater volume without a ratable increase in data processing cost. These points should not be given too much mileage—most businessmen must look at present dollar savings, not abstract advantages and projections.

This type of summary is necessary to supply management with enough information to justify its approval and backing. As in any company undertaking, management support is a requisite for successful operation of a data processing program. But backing should not be given without understanding.

Organizing for Action

If management approves continuing action toward installation of the data processing program developed in this special assignment, the operating organization can then be established.

There exists, at this point, a tremendous potential if systems work is organizationally integrated with the data processing activity. Too often, however, systems and data processing are separate operations reporting at different points and levels in the company. If we dig deeply into the problem, we will conclude that the best method is to combine the two functions. True, some procedures are not affected by data processing, but once widespread use of the equipment is a reality, there will be few of these exceptions. And, if the integration concept is sold and a single function is organized, the perplexing problems of interorganization rivalry and suspicion will be more easily overcome.

Many will claim that the controller, or the top financial executive, should be responsible for data processing. This opinion has good reason for existence. Accountants were the first big users of data processing equipment. Therefore, even people outside the profession sometimes accede to this seemingly preëmptive right to administer the operation. Nor have accountants themselves questioned this right. Too often, they have leaned back to enjoy it.

Some top financial executives have, in the past, given too little attention to directing data processing. Responsibility has been assigned at low levels, and the function has been allowed to run itself. In many cases this has led to the removal of data processing from the financial organization; in others, such a change is an ever-present and at times a well-deserved threat.

There are those who will claim the accountant has done much to improve the state of the data processing art. This is true of some, but more often the art has flourished in spite of him. Too often the accountant in charge of data processing has spent his days explaining why things could not be done. He could always, as a last resort, lean on the staff of conformity or take up his bludgeon—consistency. He applied consistency not only to accounting problems but to every other facet of the business. And "consistency" included doing things the same old way, in accounting and elsewhere. Obviously, the application of consistency to every human undertaking would mean that nothing would ever be changed.

Realistically, we must admit that some consistency intelligently applied has merit in any profession, and that in the public accounting world certain iron-clad postulates and accounting principles are needed to protect the investing public from dishonest and careless practices. Sadly, however, many accountants have allowed their love and practice of consistency in accounting procedures to retard progress in other areas to which they have no right to apply fixed rules.

This discussion is certainly not meant to malign the accounting profession; rather, it is intended to examine the validity of the idea that any one profession, as such, is singularly qualified to rule uncontested, regardless of service given, over the data processing domain. In one case, for example, delegating responsibility for the program to the accounting organization was a mistake of major proportions. This data processing department reported six levels down in the company and four levels down in the controller's organization. Both the accountant in charge of the data processing activity and this man's superior were too poorly prepared and too uninformed for such responsibility. Actually, in this case, there was no selection— it was an automatic ascension based on position in the chain of command, not on merit.

These men completely stifled the data processing program. They did not understand any management problem that could not be itemized on a 14-column worksheet. By their insistence on a mixture of conformance and consistency, or just plain "We've always done it that way," they not only discouraged the use of data processing equipment in servicing the needs of other business activities but also maneuvered to insure that their inherent position was not encroached upon. Their weapons—statistics.

The accountant and his superior inflated data processing research costs. They "proved" their claim with figures based on myth instead of fact. Unhappily, management was not informed enough to argue with their report, which showed that a material control application on data processing equipment would indeed cost money instead of adding to profit. And, unfortunately, there was no "day in court" to refute the fiction. These men were "experts."

On the other hand, many accountants who are administrators of data processing programs have performed excellently. If he is operation-oriented and properly trained, particularly in cost accounting, the accountant makes an unusually knowledgeable systems man. It is almost axiomatic that heavy cost accounting experience is a good base on which to build administrative capability in data processing. The man with genuine cost accounting experience will have been exposed to almost every operational problem in the business. He will have a good knowledge of material control and related procedures. He will have come in contact with complex manufacturing problems and will recognize their relation to ultimate fiscal results. It is this important point that must be considered in the selection of data processing management; the men must understand the relationship of operations to profit production. They should be cognizant of the entanglements of government regulations and the effect of procedures on tax liability. The informed accountant is normally in the best position to fulfill these requirements.

There is no need, obviously, to extol further the virtues of the qualified accountant. He may be the only man in an organization who is knowledgeable about data processing and qualified to run the operation. He may not be. The choice should be based on qualification, not default.

The "ideal" organization would seem to call for consolidating systems and data processing by establishing a special vice presidency; this might include responsibility for the management of service-type functions—systems and procedures, data processing, communications (telephone, telegraph, mail, and so on), printing and reproduction, records retention, office equipment management, industrial engineering (including plant layout), industrial relations, and other similar activities. This list would of course vary from one company to another.

However, whether the man in charge of data processing is called vice president of administration, controller, or vice president for finance is not really important. It is important that wherever this man reports, it be at a level high enough to insure acceptance of his ideas, policies, and decisions. Moreover, even if we were able to bring about such a grouping of all the service functions under a vice president of administration, the problem of grouping those functions most closely related to our subject would still be present.

We are concerned here only with good data processing management. Which of the service functions best fit into our plans? Which will allow the most intelligent utilization of equipment and people in the area of our interest?

Let us therefore allocate the responsibility for systems and procedures, programing, data processing operations, and communications to a man upon whom we confer some such descriptive title as "manager, information systems." For simplicity, we shall refer to him as the "data processing manager." Our suggested combination of functions will give this manager the tools to coordinate, design, and describe systems and to receive, produce, collect, and transmit information by mechanized means. But how do we select a man who knows how to use these tools intelligently?

This man, like the top executive, should be profit-oriented; he should have a broad knowledge of the company's operations and its fiscal problems; and, most important, he should have proven ability as a problem solver. He should possess the ability to sell. He must first sell himself to his organization and to the rest of the company. Then he must be able to sell his organization to the company for the difficult "trial and prove" period. The right kind of data processing manager must also have an awareness that his is a service organization, and that the added power he is given by delegation of systems and procedures, if improperly used, will result in his downfall and, further, may well lead to the destruction of whatever headway the company has made in the development of machine systems.

*Point all the players on the team toward their common goal;
be sure all are using the same rule book; and insist on the
Magna Carta of data processing.*

5. Getting in Motion

OUR ATTENTION TO THIS POINT HAS FOCUSED ON THE GENERAL
questions of equipment and organization. This has been a necessary
preliminary to discussing operations and operating management
problems because it is in these areas that a data processing program
is first guaranteed success or permanently doomed to failure.

To continue, let us assume that the decision has been made to
overhaul present systems, whether already mechanized or hand-
operated. The systems approach varies little in either case, since
the real job lies in making a change from present practices. The only
major difference, one which will be discussed later, is that the need
for training and education is more critical where hand systems are
being used. Even this, however, varies in degree depending on the
type of program proposed.

Starting Up

We shall assume that the man who was previously assigned to study
the use of data processing equipment has submitted his final report
to top management and that the questions of equipment type,
manning, and facility were considered in the computation of savings
before the decision was made to pursue the program.

These elements of equipment type, manning, and facility must,
of course, be considered in such a preliminary study. Procuring equipment sometimes takes months, the machine room must be set up if
one is not already available, and hiring and training programs must
be started. If data processing equipment is already in use, and if
equipment, people, and facility are set, the job is much easier; but
the preliminary survey will still be necessary to determine that this
is so.

The problem is a simultaneous equation—do systems precede

selection of machines or vice versa? The systems purist would claim we must know what the system will be before we can select the correct machine. Practically speaking, however, what we can afford will always influence our decision about what we will acquire and often will determine our operating limits.

The major machine considerations, other than basic economics, will be sequence and volume of processing; these determinations can be made in the preliminary studies. In further rebuff to the purist's argument, it seems wise to review some of the basic equipment questions, answers to which will have added to the accuracy of decisions reached in the selection of equipment.

1. Do systems require random or direct access to data—that is, direct access without search of tape or cards—or can data best be processed sequentially?
2. Is a combination of random and sequential data to be processed? If so, what is the weight of each in the total requirement?
3. What is the total volume and time load as determined in the preliminary study? Will it absorb costs? (This is established by examining the costs of the various makes and models being considered to meet systems requirements.)
4. What is the future load likely to be?
5. How much extra power will be added over and above current needs to assure that the machine will be capable of handling both present and future load? How much of this can be provided by ordering equipment which is modular in design, thus avoiding the cost of advance preparation for future load?

These main factors should, of course, be considered in the preliminary study by the executive in charge, assisted by technicians. It is not our intent to imply that machine selection is to be taken lightly; rather, we suggest that the decision may be reached before systems studies are made in detail.

This is not the only approach; possibly it is not even the best one. But if management is anxious to get under way, it would do better to use this approach than to spend months on costly systems work only to find that the same intelligence could have been developed months earlier without loss of valuable time.

There will be further discussion of equipment later—these points are broached here only for the purpose of explaining what otherwise might be misinterpreted as a perilous method of machine selection. With all the industry machine experience we have to draw upon— some 200 computers are already on the market, including foreign makes—there is a wealth of reliable information available to use in selecting data processing equipment.

The Magna Carta for Systems Success

Regardless of type or make of equipment to be ordered, top management will now have selected the point of responsibility for data processing, be it the controller, the vice president for finance, the vice president of administration, or any other. The data processing manager will then have been appointed, reporting directly to the top man selected. If this chain of command is not adopted, he should report no lower than do other operating managers with whom he will deal, or perhaps it should be said that he should report no higher. Equal footing with the other managers is preferable, since it is more palatable to everyone. Something like the reporting relationship shown in the accompanying exhibit may be used as a model.

When the jobs have been defined and the men have been chosen to fill them, an official announcement should be made to the organization, giving the data processing organization its charter. But if he is realistic, the data processing manager will not expect the organization to be overly anxious at this point to assist him with the job of mechanized system development. Not at all. On the contrary, he is more likely to be classed as a threat to the status quo; a despot who will even offer the employees as sacrifices to what they view as another kingdom, an automated autonomy. If he is not the right kind of manager, they will be correct in their view.

Should employee antagonism grow, intraorganizational conferences may conceivably be held on how to frustrate the data processing manager's plans, seemingly in complete defiance of stated management policy. Or the objectors may not use open defiance; they can achieve the same results with an unorganized, but extremely effective, passive resistance movement—chipping away at little errors in planning, picking at small points, and withholding needed information.

Because these things can and do happen in some organizations, the

DATA PROCESSING'S PLACE IN THE COMPANY STRUCTURE

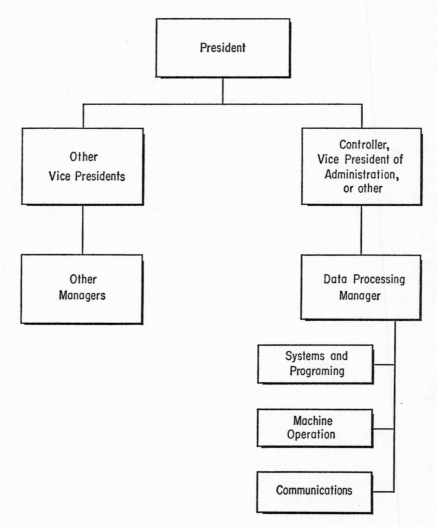

problem of operating management acceptance is the second big hurdle which must be cleared before satisfactory progress will be made. But there is a solution to the problem. It lies in asking the affected managers to participate in the systems description; to help in preparing a simple, yet complete, synopsis in laymen's terms of the plan and how it will affect their departments and their men. They should play an important role in this task, even if it slows down the data processing manager or hurts his pride of authorship.

This synopsis will be the master plan for data processing. It will be the guide for the systems people and therefore must be complete enough to answer pertinent questions. It should be explicit enough to allow the designers to define the desired output; it should contain subtle references to cutting organizational lines, including the best possible methods, abhorrence of duplicate records, and—particularly important—the points where responsibility is placed. It should have the qualities of a "timeless" document—a Magna Carta of data processing, if you will.

A table of contents for the Magna Carta might be as follows:

1. A general statement of the goals and objectives of the system, featuring avoidance of duplication.

2. The affected organizations and an outline of their responsibilities.

3. A broad description of what results are expected from the completed system.

4. Background information on why the system is necessary, giving sufficient detail to promote adequate understanding of the need.

5. A summary of savings expected, listed by phases of installation if in more than one phase.

6. General procedure and policy to be followed in the installation of each phase, setting out responsibilities at the operating levels.

7. Comments on coding to be used and the necessity for the tie-in of coding with other jobs related indirectly to the one described; for example, accounts payable and material systems as they concern the use of material code numbers.

8. A discussion of problems likely to be encountered in the future and an exhortation to provide flexibility in anticipation of unknown requirements.

9. A schedule of installation dates by phases (or parts), sufficiently broken down to allow surveillance of schedule position.

10. General closing remarks: assurances that the write-up is to state policy and general procedures, that it is not meant to detail procedures, and that systems people may use judgment within the framework of policy statements.

11. Signatures of managers and top management.

The very preparation of such a document will bear fruit: It will add to the data processing manager's understanding of the eventual system; it will inform the other managers about the plan; and it will help achieve general agreement before system design or revision is begun. This document will be the battle armor; it will defeat all subsequent obstacles if it is properly prepared.

After a satisfactory plan has been achieved, all the affected managers should approve it along with the data processing manager. Top management must then approve it to assure maximum effectiveness. The information that is contained in the write-up—the Magna Carta—will clear away those bottlenecks that result from organizational disagreements, the major deterrent to successful completion of systems work.

Don't keep the management view a secret; eliminate the guessing game by preparing terse, succinct statements of policy on information systems.

6. Top Management Push

To AVOID MISUNDERSTANDING ON WHAT CAN EASILY BECOME A MOST confusing subject, it seems appropriate here to review the steps considered thus far in the installation or overhaul of a data processing program.

1. Initiate the preliminary study to decide whether to pursue the idea further.
2. Give the special assignment to a member of top management if possible. In any case, relieve the person selected of all line duties during the study. He will develop written plans on areas offering savings—describe, compute savings, and so on—then submit his report to top management.
3. If the plan is approved, select the man to head up the information program (vice president of administration, controller, or other).
4. Select the data processing manager. He will prepare the Magna Carta for each major system area and secure the approval both of managers at his own level and of superiors.

Statement of Policy on Systems

We make no claim that the method here discussed is the only way to approach the problem. This method should, however, be of particular interest where the expenditure for such an undertaking is critical, because the program may be stopped at three checkpoints before large sums of money are expended. This is made possible because top management is itself accountable for the first three decisions—the critical points in the program which require the heavy push from sources of authority.

The outline of the Magna Carta in Chapter 5 deserves further attention at this point in evaluating management responsibility. Does the outline seem to be idealistic and to deal in the obvious?

51

Even the experienced executive may be surprised to find on investigation that a data processing program is constantly threatened by evasions of what he would consider plain, everyday logic.

Does the outline seem to contain too little description, not enough detail? Here lies another threat. Too much detail will destroy the intent and will lead to misinterpretation; for the greater the detail, the better the chance to abort the outline's real purpose. As an analogy, consider the Biblical injunction that we should not kill. No qualifying phrases have been added; we have not been told, for example, that we should not kill except in self-defense. If this had been written in, the human mind would find some way to rationalize every murder and justify self-forgiveness.

The write-up of the Magna Carta should state systems objectives clearly and concisely, carefully avoiding any statements that allow alternative interpretations. At the same time it must permit freedom of action within the bounds of reason; for, without this freedom, the systems man would be hamstrung. The Magna Carta is a broad systems description. It should, above all things, be a simple statement of management goals. And implicit in this statement must be top management support of systems, for systems without policy guidance are useless, or worse. In fact, systems cannot be designed properly without policy guidance; they will not stand the test of time.

The Magna Carta is a written policy statement in specific areas of system work. Even if unwritten policy is developed by one individual, good communication might help define it so clearly that the same results could be achieved. However, this is testing chance, especially where turnover of personnel may bring not only new faces but changes in unwritten policy by gradual erosion of management's original intent.

Therefore, a top management which seeks to achieve maximum efficiency in systems will perform one more very important act— the preparation of a policy statement on all reporting systems. A sample of such a statement follows:

POLICY ON MANAGEMENT REPORTING SYSTEMS

I. *Purpose*

The purpose of this policy statement is to record basic management policies with respect to systems to be used in the operation of the business, and in reporting on these operations.

II. *General Policy*

Although the company operates on a decentralized basis from the standpoint of management responsibility, it will be the policy to maintain the highest degree of compatibility practicable in the area of operating and reporting systems. It will also be the policy to utilize, to the extent practicable, data processing and other equipment in the collection, handling, and dissemination of information; and to do so, wherever economically feasible, on a centralized basis so as to gain maximum utilization from equipment and personnel.

It will be the policy of the company to require design of systems to be preceded with adequate studies of the advantages and the cost savings to be gained therefrom as compared to present or alternative methods. This will be done in full consideration of the requirements of the company as a whole, rather than of individual organizational units. It follows, therefore, as part of this policy, that system design will cut across organizational lines to provide information to all organizations which require it. It will be recognized that the test of need will be the predominant consideration in the design of systems and that duplication of functions, operations, or related management action will be avoided as a specific requirement of this policy statement.

In the determination of the foregoing, there is a need for close coordination of systems effort among all organizational units. The policy will be to require such coordination regardless of the formal organizational structure of the systems functions.

III. *Data Processing Equipment Use*

It is the policy of the company to utilize equipment in the processing of data toward generation of information for management use. For the purpose of definition, data processing equipment is considered to be any equipment utilized in the processing or producing of paperwork within the company.

Upon considering the use of equipment as a means of processing data, it will ordinarily be necessary to review the capabilities of more than one make or type. In some cases, to be specifically determined, it may be the policy to standardize on a particular make or model for reasons of overall efficiency or because of maintenance considerations. In all cases, however, equipment will be used only where it will furnish, both economically and expeditiously, required systems support for undertakings in harmony with descriptions stated under Article II. General Policy.

Data processing equipment (EDPM and EAM) is utilized throughout the company. Organizational units have been formed for the specific purpose of operating the equipment, and such equipment may not be procured or operated outside the bounds of specified organizations. This equipment will include, but is not necessarily limited to, EAM (electric accounting machines) punched card processors and EDPM (electronic data processing machines) which use cards or magnetic tapes.

Some of the basic rules to be followed in the use of large-scale data processing equipment are:

1. Equipment will be used to the fullest extent practicable before ordering additional equipment. If it appears necessary to order additional equipment, studies will be made of existing workloads to evaluate the overload, including investigations into the use and utility of reports. Whether the overload is temporary or permanent will be determined and, if it is temporary, the possibility of utilizing outside services will be considered.

2. Jobs will be matched to machines to assure that the full capability of the equipment is used.

3. Although computers have the ability to check the accuracy or reliability of input from manual sources, and although some of this checking is desirable, it is the policy of the company to require safeguards against carelessness in the preparation of input, thereby not relying wholly on the machines to detect errors. Input systems will therefore be designed to produce fully balanced and otherwise reliable data for the computer. Self-checking features will be used in the computer programs but will be limited to significant control checks. Machine systems will not be used as a crutch for poor systems input. Responsibility for accuracy of reports in this respect will rest with management charged with the duty of proper input.

4. Requests for special jobs will be evaluated to determine whether alternative methods will furnish the desired information or substantially satisfactory data at a lower cost without use of the computer. Special requests will require high management approval before they will be processed on large-scale data processing equipment.

5. Systems will not be computerized until they are properly documented, programed, and checked out in accordance with the rules of system development spelled out in Article II. General Policy. Likewise, no job will be discontinued without approval by all management involved directly or indirectly in the use of the information generated by the report.

6. Records of machine usage will be kept and cost and machine usage reports will be made monthly, classified by jobs.

7. Scientific (engineering) computing will be performed on an

"open shop" basis, but jobs will be cleared through an engineering computer coordinator who will control and catalogue
scientific programs and routines to assure that duplication of
effort will not result.

8. Management will assign a point of responsibility charged
with evaluation, try-outs, procurement, maintenance, and
other logistic duties related to all data processing equipment.

IV. *Application of Policy*

It will be the responsibility of all management levels to carry
out the policies established herein and to make decisions on items
not specifically covered in this statement by applying sound business judgment which will be in general harmony with the intent
and purposes stated herein.

It will be the policy to require not only that studies be made to
determine the advantages and the cost savings to be gained in
the installation of systems, but that programs be coordinated
with the budget department to assure that predicted cost savings
do in fact come about. These savings will be reflected in revised
budgets for the organizations involved.

Approved:

_____

_____

(Signatures of top management)

Relation of Policy and Systems

It is common to hear systems personnel referred to just as if they
were bricklayers or carpenters. Want ads read: "Business systems men
needed." An executive refers to the people in a certain area as "our
systems department." We even hear the title "systems engineer" used
in describing businessman and scientist alike. One can become confused as to the real meaning of systems and the classification of systems personnel.

All logical people are systems-oriented. In every act of living there
is a system involved. That some systems are carefully thought out

and some are bungled shows that even in the business of living there are good planners and poor ones.

Without becoming too philosophical over the matter, it should be mentioned that certain basic rules of life govern our systems of physical behavior and that straying too far from these will ruin our health. In the operation of a business, likewise, and particularly in the design of a business system, basic rules must be set down if the business is to remain healthy. These rules compose the company's policy statement.

This may sound elementary and even crass to one who is accustomed to such glamorous modern management techniques as operations research, PERT, and mathematical models. But however successful the search for new methods of management, the top man will be hard-pressed to dodge his primary responsibility—to set and administer policy.

Most companies do not design data processing systems; instead, they put together machine procedures. There is a tremendous difference between the two; a difference brought about by lack of management policy in systems design.

In one case, the problem was to analyze rejections made by quality control people, to furnish information that would help prevent recurrences, and to grade vendors. There were no policy statements, no Magna Carta written by interested management—just a need to do the job. The systems people and programers set about developing a system. The original intent was to provide the bit of information deemed to be important to the quality control department, but the system ended up furnishing detailed data to many other functions. The primary criterion used by the systems man was: "If it's available, make a report on it." The system grew and grew to the point that the report originally asked for was a minor portion of the output. The other reports were full of information, but no one had requested it, no one used it, and, furthermore, no one really wanted it. But, in order to keep in step with the so-called data management program, the useless reports were accepted and filed away each week.

The systems man should, of course, be alert to find useful innovations when designing a system and should test stated policy to assure that the formally expressed intent remains unchallenged. This is no suggestion that blind adherence to policy should be practiced, but neither is it a proposal that the systems man should set policy while designing a system. In the absence of stated policy—in writing or otherwise—the setting of policy is justified by the need for decision about system design.

The systems man cannot be blamed for lack of policy, nor can he be criticized too severely for excesses in design because of it. The blame falls on the data processing manager for not insisting on policy guidance, and on top management for failing to provide it in the first place.

7. Budgets or Bludgeons

Budgets are wonderful tools for management control. No rational person would argue that such an undertaking as a data processing program should not be budgeted. There is, however, a tendency to go too far and too deep with budgeting—to require too much detail. And there is another point on which no two men will agree completely: Should budgets be administered at the lowest level of supervision, at the manager's level, or at the vice president's level? There is no pat answer to this question; it depends on the size of the organization, its products, and—probably most impelling—the profit position. This facet of budgeting clearly is not our subject here, but we must find a sensible way to control data processing costs, especially during the critical installation period.

Budgeting Data Processing R&D

Some companies charge research and development cost directly to the managers who will ultimately benefit from the installation of the system, prorating the cost in one manner or another to those areas while the developmental work is under way. Not only is this a useless and inaccurate method, but it makes enemies for the program, and at a high level. The manager of the material department, as an example, has to buy, store, issue, and report on his activity. While development is in progress, he is getting nothing from data processing except more work, and adding R&D charges to his current expenditures is like waving a red flag at an already angry bull.

Though this may seem relatively unimportant, it causes many a program to be scuttled before it starts. Why? Simply because a budget report can be two feet long and the vice president, the executive vice president, the president, and the board look only at the bottom figure. Remove the body of the budget report and they no doubt will notice its absence, but they still tend to skip right to the last line.

Let's face up to it. Whether we show the added cost of development in the body of the report or show it at the bottom separately, excluded from the total, top management may not see the reason for the budget increase but may see only the fact that there has been an increase.

Even if management does not notice the development cost figure, the harassed department manager will. If he is truly a good manager, he will suffer pangs of self-torment for allowing this cost to be heaped on top of his present expenditures. And even though the expense may have been approved by the highest executive, he will still be apprehensive.

A better way to handle the problem is to make up a separate budget sheet for the data processing development cost and call it "business methods research and development," as it actually is just that. Break it down by projects, not by departments. Since a business system should cut across organizational lines, how can we intelligently charge it to departments?

At this juncture, we have a problem in trying to line up the constituents for the big job ahead. We should therefore make it especially clear to the managers involved that this is a companywide project and that the several departments will not be charged directly with the development costs. By doing this, we will have made friends and influenced people—the kind we need at this point. It does not cost any more, and flogging a dead horse does not get a load moved.

Budgeting of Operations

If everyone who is concerned with data processing is turned loose to do as he pleases with the equipment, the result may resemble a "painting" created by framing the artist's palette. Don't be surprised if some data processing systems are found to be similarly concocted. A data processing system that looks good on the surface may prove to be a costly, confused conglomeration when we dig deeper. What has this to do with operating budgets? Nothing directly, of course, but budgets can do much to compound the problem of patches on patches.

A good budget program will not allow scientific research and development money to be spent without executive approval; why, then, should large amounts be allowed for data processing projects without advance approval? The dollars are just as green. Good systems planning should set out the goals of the proposed program and include a cost estimate for implementation—the R&D cost we have discussed. It should also set out an estimate of the savings to be realized when the equipment is installed. These estimates—and this is quite important—must be acknowledged and agreed to by the parties involved.

A copy of the plans, including dates for equipment installation as well as figures, should be sent to the budget department for future reference. When the plan is installed, the budget should be revised to reduce the allocation for the benefiting departments and increase the data processing allocation. Naturally the two amounts should not be the same, since we expect the machine methods to save money.

Why not charge back the cost of the new system and let the net savings accrue to the benefiting department's record? A good question—but should the credit and the financial benefits that accrue as a result of the change to a data processing system go only to one department? Aren't they the result of companywide effort? And shouldn't both credit and benefits be reported to reflect this?

It may be claimed that when a departmental budget is reduced to reflect the savings from computer operation, the benefiting manager is right back where he started. But the fact is that his budget is based on what he should spend, and with new service he should spend less.

The Scourge of the Charge-Back Budget System

Many recommend that data processing service costs be charged back to the benefiting departments. Nevertheless, we believe the charge-back system is a major deterrent to a sensible data processing program.

The charge-back system was developed in the early days of data processing when everyone was arguing over what should be done with the machines. Finally it was decided that each function should be given a free hand to develop its own internal systems, but in doing so each would incur a direct charge against its budget. The rules of fair play also included the postulate that no one department would step over the boundaries of any other. In that way each could keep its own kingdom intact. Happily uneducated in the details of data processing, top management seldom looked to see what was happening; it believed the use of data processing equipment was in itself proof of progress. So, said those responsible, why not engage in a little skullduggery over costs and charges? Everyone was doing it.

If the R&D part of the data processing program is treated as a companywide project—that is, if we refrain from charging the cost back to individual budgets—we can avoid developing and operating parallel systems for different departments when a single system could do the job. To avoid duplication, we cut across organizational lines wherever possible. But, if the systems are companywide and the budgeting is departmental—that is, using the charge-back system—we are in many cases telling the unhappy manager of Department X, for example, "Yes, we are now charging you for work in the data processing system that formerly was done in Department Y." And how do we charge back the cost of a report which goes to several departments? Should the charge be divided equally among all the users? We can do this, but how accurate will such an allocation of cost be and what use is it after it's done?

According to the charge-back philosophy, whoever asks for something pays for it. This puts the responsibility for a project on the instigator, and no matter which department uses it thereafter, the instigating department bears the cost. So, even if someone else tries to modify it in a way that will accomplish more and will show big companywide savings, the user can block any improvement by refusing to accept the resulting charges against his budget. This is ridiculous, and yet it happens in many large companies that use data processing equipment. Why? Because too few executives can put over the idea that systems must be developed on a companywide basis and installed to do the best possible job without regard for organizational lines. This takes not only intestinal fortitude but power, and the power can come from one place only—the top. Unfortunately, because of other pressures, the top man is not usually close to the problem. And, without his direction, the next level of management must resort to the charge-back system. "Use it all you want, but we'll see that you pay." Somehow it sounds more like a threat than anything else.

It is, of course, very important to know how and where money is being spent. Even if we are fortunate enough to avoid the charge-back system, we will still want to maintain good control and must therefore price out the jobs being done. But why should the total cost of the operation be spread over the work being done—the practice being followed by most adherents to the charge-back philosophy? This results in making a charge above or below what the job is really worth in order to have everything come out even and show, at least on paper, that the data processing department is operating at 100 per cent efficiency.

The data processing department in your organization, or the organization you are planning, should, from the viewpoint of results, be considered a service function, much like the service bureaus you can hire in any large city. These bureaus must price jobs competitively in order to stay in business—unless they are a monopoly, which your department may fancy itself to be. Why not price jobs out on a realistic basis and see that your installation is absorbing the cost? Even if you still use the charge-back system, costs can be applied on a fixed price basis with the variance from total going to the credit or discredit of the data processing activity.

Better still, summarize the jobs being done by areas of accounting, material, and the like, and report to top management on total cost and cost being absorbed by jobs or new developments; however, do your budgeting at the data processing department level. Should you need information for assigning costs to specific overhead pools or groups for accounting reasons, this can be done by proration, which will probably be more accurate than charge-backs. If your procedures call for charge-backs, think the whole system over and determine what it is doing for you—or against you. Accurately appraised, the practice will prove—we confidently believe—to be stifling real progress.

Getting things done in the information program will ultimately depend on the quality of the people in the data processing group. Be sure they are up to the task and organized properly.

8. The Data Processing Department

THE DATA PROCESSING MANAGER, AS WE HAVE DESCRIBED HIS JOB, HAS three major areas of responsibility: design of systems, programing or machine instruction, and operations. If his is a large installation, he will set up a fourth area—the administrative function—to order and issue supplies, type procedures, control and distribute reports, and perform similar services. A small organization may find it more economical to split these administrative functions among the other three or to have some of them handled by the manager's staff. A typical organization is shown in the accompanying exhibit. Let us consider these phases of the data processing department's job in the order in which they occur.

Systems People—and Getting Things Done

In manning the systems organization we are interested not so much in a high degree of machine understanding as in a well-rounded knowledge of company operations. Where size demands it, systems can be split into groups such as manufacturing, material, and general business services—including, for example, accounting and business administration in the engineering department. These groupings should not be considered rigid criteria, for obviously an insurance company will have neither manufacturing nor material but may need to divide general services into three separate areas. In any case the groups should be highly coordinated, reporting to a single individual.

Regardless of differences in the applicability of systems in varying situations, the salient point is that they be established in conformity with the intent of the Magna Carta, the written plan which management will previously have prepared, agreed to, and distributed. By studying this document, the systems man will be able to determine what is expected of him.

ORGANIZATION CHART FOR THE DATA PROCESSING DEPARTMENT

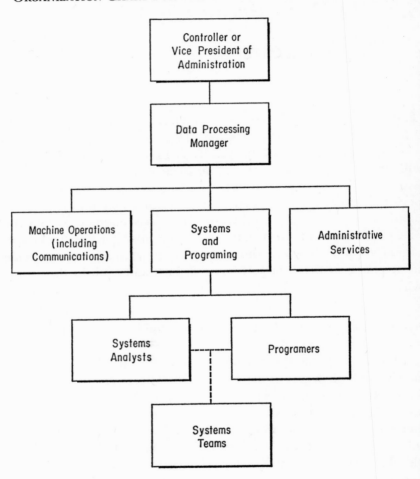

What other steps can we take to assure that systems work will progress satisfactorily? Problems of an internal nature in the data processing organization can be dealt with by the manager. However, "foreign" relations are a different matter. Though it may sound trite to expound on developing healthy attitudes in systems people, this must nevertheless be accomplished. And it can be done by reminding the systems man that the department's duty is to provide service, not to establish servitude through automation. Many data processing programs are failures because the need for this very important management influence is not recognized.

The data processing manager will also be wise to establish firm official contact points. He should insist on appointment of a specific person in each area—the most knowledgeable person available—with whom the data processing systems man will work. Each should be instructed to coordinate all action with the other. This will place responsibility at both ends so that progress can be measured.

After all this, the data processing manager is still treading on marshy ground, for he is ultimately responsible, through his systems people, for seeking out areas where work should be removed from one department and done in another, if at all. His duty in this regard may have been stated in the Magna Carta, but there is, of course, a difference between making rules and enforcing them. The data processing manager should therefore instruct his systems people to avoid useless arguments on controversial subjects, and to attempt to anticipate them and discuss them within the department first. The more important matters can then be referred to the data processing manager's superior so that he may decide the steps to be taken in approaching an argumentative issue. The top executive may find it appropriate to discuss the more important matters with the executive concerned, thus effecting a solution painlessly at a high level. This is desirable in many cases; still, much care should be taken that lower management prerogatives are not unnecessarily usurped in such a process.

It is evident that, in the business of installing successful data systems, top management will occasionally be obliged to provide the necessary punch—even in areas often regarded as routine. As in the early part of the program, top management push will be especially helpful, where roadblocks appear, in keeping the systems task from slowing down. The top executive must allocate time for reviewing the methods proposed in attacking systems problems, checking on adherence to schedules, and, importantly, reviewing estimates on installation costs and savings.

As in any other major undertaking there is value, economically as well as politically, in picking certain parts of the overall program which can be made to pay off quickly. Whether a company is already using card equipment and is now switching to a computer, or whether it is just acquiring its first data processing equipment, rapid progress can be made with a minimum of conflict with later installations and with little chance of damage to the eventual integration of systems.

Accounting routines are mechanically easy to install, not because they are artless but because normal numerical coding is sometimes usable with little change. And because accounting is under the control of a localized group, rapid decisions and quick installation are possible once the idea is sold.

A payroll is a good example of a job that may well be installed first. Payroll is a "bread and butter" job or, more properly, an overhead absorption job. We should not expect machine processing of a big payroll to result in major cost improvement, but if the distribution of labor costs is added, the returns will usually be gratifying. Moreover, if the payroll and personnel records are combined (a possibility that will require real selling), very handsome dividends in clerical cost savings will result in both the payroll and the personnel departments.

Accounts payable may be considered another accounting job with potential for quick returns, but if the machines are used only for disbursing or scheduling payments, the results will usually be disappointing. If there is a distribution problem—that is, a question about where to charge payments—incorporating this in the system will produce savings, though probably in small amounts. If such a system is designed to fit into an integrated budget program covering other, related needs such as small business reports required by the government, the payoff is always increased substantially.

As a general rule, we should not rely on accounting projects for more than nominal savings and quick overhead recovery, unless the business is largely of that type—for example, an insurance company or public utility.

It is in the manufacturing and product marketing industries that inventory and manufacturing control systems become big money savers. These will be recognized as long-range projects, but even so, we should not submit to the argument that it will take five years to complete the typical installation in these areas. The proper organizational approach to systems will begin to produce gratifying results in a short time span, measured in proportion to management leadership through active participation.

Organization for Effective Programing

The exhibit that appears early in this chapter shows systems analysts and programers reporting to a head of systems and programing. The purpose of this organizational arrangement is to assure close coordination and teamwork where systems cut across departmental lines or depend on one another.

To illustrate another important reason for close association, take the example of Company X, a manufacturing concern using large-scale computers. "Over here are our programers; across the way, our systems analysts," the tour guide points out with pride. You gaze around the room, nodding your head affirmatively, but always your eyes return to the great wide aisle dividing the room.

"I notice you're wondering about the openness of our quarters. We have no walls because the analysts and programers must communicate."

Again you nod your head in appreciation of the explanation, but you go on wondering if they can really communicate across this imaginary Maginot Line.

After the tour you will still be trying to visualize how information is supposed to flow from one set of specialists (the analysts) to the other group (the programers) in this immense room with the wide aisle down the middle. You are not particularly awed by the fact that the company has been able to gather so much talent but are more interested in how they are directed.

The philosophy in many large companies is that one must overpower the job by hiring large numbers of people. Coupled with the idea that programers and systems people should be isolated in their respective groups and should even have separate supervision, this actually creates a barrier to progress as well as a horrendous increase in costs.

To be sure, the practice is commonly accepted. And the normality of the decision to separate the two groups is unquestionable, particularly where pay scales are such that management hesitates to mix them for fear of an explosion. But, even where this is a real-life problem, the volatile qualities will surely be increased by marked segregation. The systems analyst creates, and the programer puts his creation into a language that will be understood by the computer. This is what the purist in data processing organization would claim, and who would argue with this generalization? But is it proper to put the systems group on a project basis and generalize in programer assignment?

If we were to apply a strict policy of segregation, we would assign analysts to develop a system and furnish flow charts, coding, and other documentation; then we would select programers to put these plans into the computer. The project would naturally look like all the others to the programer, and he would attack it with the impersonal interest of a ditch digger. Seeking recognition, he might resort to criticizing the documentation, or he might do things just as they were depicted even though he was quite aware of errors in the charted flow. He might even try to embarrass the analyst by building in complications which did not exist or by dragging his feet to make the system and the schedule look ridiculous. Programers are human; when segregated, they will strike out against the system every time for one simple reason: They are computerizing a creation in which they have had no part.

This is the reason for the proposed blending of systems and programing wherein each project is assigned to a specific group which combines both skills under one capable supervisor. Under this arrangement the analyst should review each system with the programers at regular intervals even though the programers may be actively engaged on other projects. Also, the systems men should be acquainted with general programing problems and, if time allows, programers should do a bit of systems work. Against all the rules of good data processing organization? Not so.

Scheduling the Programing Work

The assignment of systems and programing to one supervisor under the data processing manager will add another very important organizational ingredient; that is, the ability to schedule and to monitor schedules.

A few years back we did not fret about schedules or overly concern ourselves with the care and feeding of data processing people. This does not mean we were not appreciative of the remarkable job performed by our erstwhile organization and punched card equipment;

but, compared with today's technical problems and high costs, life was then relatively relaxed and simple. If someone in the machine room quit, we took it philosophically and hired another worker without undue emotion. If we had trouble getting a replacement, we ran the equipment ourselves until we found one. At that time it seemed to be stylish for the president to occasionally run a sorter or to feed cards into the printer while it wrote checks. It was fun.

Now, even if the executive is allowed in the computer room, he would never dare touch a thing lest he upset an entire month's work. He is frightened by the equipment and awed by the people who operate it. Most of his reverence is, however, reserved for the supernal inhabitant of the data processing world—the programer.

Programers come in assorted sizes, colors, and creeds. They are of both sexes—women are firmly entrenched in this profession. Programers may be pleasant or unpleasant, spineless or aggressive, according to their own choosing, their experience, and how badly someone wants their services.

To some executives in the front office, a programer is a programer and the only difference among them, other than sex, is the amount of money they are being paid. These executives have created a visual image which portrays all programers. And some of them view this portrait with fear.

Why is this? The programer does not enjoy being looked upon as a freak or as one who talks in unknown tongues. He has the normal desire for recognition. He aspires to advancement in the company and hopes that someday he may become a respected member of management.

Recently someone remarked, "You can't schedule programing work. It involves too much research—it's an art, not a science. Besides, when you try to force a schedule on a programer, he considers it regimentation and you are very likely to lose him."

Such a blanket statement about programers as a group or as a whole is nonsense. Certainly there are times when programers may be engaged in art and creation, the R&D type of work which cannot be pinned to precise schedules. But, generally speaking, programers, like any other group, do not meet schedules when they are not given schedules to meet—in which case management will indeed have a roomful of artists using their inventiveness for the benefit of posterity —slowly.

It is admittedly difficult to schedule programing work. But even so, if a system is developed and flow-charted first, it is possible to determine the extent of the programing task. Once the number of programs is established, an experienced man can determine the relative complexity of each one and estimate the time necessary to do the job. Then, when management has determined the "need" date, the number of programers required can be established by simple arithmetic. Like all others, however, a programing schedule must be reviewed often to establish the relation of accomplishment to time and expenditures. A good programing schedule will become a better one as time progresses. What is more, active management review can anticipate trouble and forestall it.

And what about the effect of scheduling on the programer? Contrary to widespread opinion, it will generate a feeling of belonging to an organized team with an important job to do. As the industrial psychologists already know, most people—including programers—require deadlines to work against; they actually welcome them as a personal yardstick and a much-needed source of job satisfaction.

For Better Machine Operations

The machine operations group is the one charged with the repetitive jobs after they are set up and programed. Of particular importance here is the word "repetitive." No job should be assigned to the machine room until it is completely tested and has been proved to operate successfully. This rule requires rigorous attention on the part of the data processing manager. He must insist on a high level of cooperation during the checkout period to assure that operations will make machine time conveniently available to the programer and will stand by also as an apprentice. Operations may be compared to the student who is learning to fly—only when he is ready will his solo flight be made. Just so, only when the job is ready and the operations people are sufficiently checked out should sole responsibility for the job be transferred and the procedure become a repetitive duty.

When transfer is not made cleanly, the systems and programing personnel may be tied to a job forevermore. If the job has not been properly documented with detailed system write-ups, charts, and program listings, we can expect trouble in completing the transfer of responsibility. And the end result may well be that both operations and systems and programing ultimately become a polyglot with each group vying for leadership in directing the confusion. This is a common malady and one of the biggest reasons for high costs as well as for schedule failures in systems installation.

One other caution seems appropriate and necessary. The quality of personnel in operations should not be downgraded to secondary importance, as is often done. The supervisor of the machine operations group should be just as capable and knowledgeable in his field as the head of systems and programing.

The head of operations may or may not be in charge of keypunch and communications equipment, but it seems best to localize all machines under the operations head. Such an arrangement allows management to insist on better utilization of equipment and affords operations the opportunity to innovate in the use of the machines when there is down time. Better utilization of employee time may thus be achieved; as an example, keypunch operators may be capable of performing other machine operations during slack periods.

The Administrative Services Group

Listed here are some of the functions under the administrative services group.

Logistics	Services	Administrative
Supply ordering	Typing	Control and distribution of reports
Issue of supplies	Secretarial	
Tape testing and certification	Filing	Balancing of reports
	Clerical	Master file maintenance
		Tape control
		Machine usage reports
		Approval of bills

Let us consider each in its turn.

Under logistics three examples are listed. The importance of the first two is apparent; there is no need to elaborate on the results of a failure to order or issue a supply of blank checks in sufficient quantities to make up a payroll, for instance.

Magnetic tape testing, the third logistics item, may be performed on equipment especially designed for the purpose or on the computer (this is called, by some, main-frame tape testing). If the computer is used—an expensive method—a specially designed routine tests all the "spots." New tapes are commonly certified for use by the manufacturer and not tested, but it may be found desirable to "sample inspect" them before they are used. Old tapes can sometimes be re-used, but they will eventually need to be cleaned and buffed smooth to eliminate bad spots, which cause much trouble. And it is as a result of tests that we can determine whether a tape should be rejected as unfit for further use.

The operations department may perform the tests if main-frame testing procedures are followed, but the tape should be stocked by the administrative services group. It may even be found desirable to provide the administrative services group with a tape tester, cleaner, and buffer if this is economically feasible, but whatever the arrangement, responsibility should be placed on a specific group for the handling and stocking of certified blank tape.

We should be very careful to buy reliable tape, for the difference in cost may be offset by the chaos caused when reruns have to be made because of bad spots. This does not necessarily mean that more money will be spent overall because quantity prices are often available for the best quality of tapes and, when the savings that go hand in hand with reliability are considered, the total cost is less. An opinion: Tape is either good or bad; there is no in-between.

A function somewhat related to tape testing is classified as administrative—that is, tape control. This is more than a filing function. Tapes from operations jobs are catalogued by input, program, output, tape number, and other identification as necessary and stored in a "library." Control totals are maintained to tie the tape control function closely to balancing responsibility. Control personnel are required to maintain tapes on the "grand-daddy, daddy, son" principle; that is, three generations of tape are kept so that a new tape may be reconstructed from earlier ones if something happens to destroy current records.

Tape control responsibility also encompasses the removal of old tapes to tape testing, where they can be cleaned, buffed, and tested as necessary. If this is not handled properly, tape costs will rise astronomically, as will storage requirements.

What happens if lightning strikes near the tape library? This is not so much a farfetched question as an admonishment to protect tape from electrical interference of any kind. Magnaflux equipment and the like should not be placed near tape storage. It is too big a chance to take. And what about atomic radiation? Possibly underground storage with shielding is the best answer in cases where extreme security measures are called for. Engineers must be consulted for the right answers.

The items labeled "services" (typing and similar tasks) need no explanation—these functions are performed for the entire department. Control and distribution of reports may be discussed with balancing, or accuracy assurance, as one subject. Control and distribution encompass the scheduling of jobs into operations and the delivery of reports to the proper recipients, both of which tasks are performed by the administrative services group. Controls are maintained, probably as a part of control and distribution; totals are furnished to operations, where tests are made against totals generated as programs are performed. Control procedures may also require some clerical activity in operations. For instance, totals on hours are furnished to operations by administrative services, but when money is expended, the operations group establishes another control check which is entered and carried through the entire processing cycle.

Most controls originate outside the data processing department. For example, the payroll department furnishes totals on hours to be paid, deductions, and so on. Data processing adds its totals, such as money, as the job progresses.

There is good reason to emphasize the need for control—a job not properly controlled and balanced is worse than worthless because reliance on such a report doubles the jeopardy. Any decision may be fraught with inaccuracies because of errors in human judgment; but what chance is there for a good decision if the reports on which the decision is based are wrong at the start?

The payroll rate file and the material item price file, among others, are called master files and are maintained in a "balanced" condition by administrative services personnel. Additions, deletions, and changes are under their control, and the operations staff is accountable to them for proper use of these files.

Approval of bills is a self-explanatory administrative function. Machine usage reports—another administrative function—are summations of cost by report, by "customer," or by other breakdown as desired. They have been discussed along with the general subject of budgeting a data processing program.

Somewhat briefly, then, this is the organization of the data processing department. Details have been avoided to stay within the basic aim of this book—to focus on the management problems involved in administering a data processing program.

9. Systems and Salesmanship

THIS BRINGS US BACK TO THE IMPORTANT ROLE OF THE SYSTEMS MAN IN the design and sale of the product—data processing. In short, the systems man must be a salesman. To be successful, he must have a salable product for which consumers have a need—the consumers, in this instance, being the departments or divisions that use the data processing service.

The Magna Carta has been prepared for the purpose of expressing company needs and declaring management's desire to pursue a well-organized approach to data processing systems, and a statement by management on information systems has covered the intent and purpose of overall company policy. Such documents are helpful in establishing an official management posture on the basis of which the data processing manager may operate. As implied earlier, they also give him enough rope to hang himself. Even though he has the best of backing in writing, he should be aware that, in his customers' minds, there is a fine line between service and despotism.

Alexander Pope is said to have remarked, "A little knowledge is a dangerous thing." This may be applied to the systems man: He can be a threat to a program because he has too little or too much knowledge of its detail; he may believe top management's support of the program has commissioned him with the prerogative to determine what operating management's needs may be.

Business and Individual Needs

There is a question of philosophy involved in the phrase "needs of the business" as opposed to those of individuals. A company is made up of human beings moving about through the arteries representing its activities. They are its lifeblood; but, being humans, they have differing opinions on any subject, usually in direct ratio to their numbers. However, the top management man should keep in mind that opinions at his level carry so much weight as to veto all others; thus he will establish all "business needs." The wise executive, being mindful of the danger, will be very careful about expressing his opinions lest he find himself responsible for everything. If he doesn't believe this, all he need do is ask—someone will promptly remind him of what he wrote or said days, weeks, months, or even years before.

The disease which infects a company run by carelessly vocal and opinionated management is what we have tabbed "boss-said-itis." When we ask why something is done in a particular way, we are told: "Because the boss said. . . ." Well-written policies can defeat boss-said-itis—but they are not often enough used.

Example: A large electronics company set up a specific organization to handle all data processing operations. It did not include systems but did include programing. Instead of preparing written policies on systems, the top executive spent much time conferring with the programing staff—expressing opinions—and the programers were hard at work acting upon those disconnected comments. System definition was bypassed, and the programers held belated classes to tell operations people what they would get from the installation. When asked why the system did not consider a specific need, the programers answered, "The boss said you didn't need that," or, "This procedure allows you more flexibility." Of course, too much flexibility can be rather like dumping a man in the middle of the ocean and leaving him to swim in any direction he chooses.

When someone claims a job is not being performed so as to provide flexibility, especially where it involves a computer, we had better look at the system. Someone may have been careless or had an attack of boss-said-itis. Omissions seldom provide flexibility; on the contrary, the right kind of flexibility is usually built in by adding something. For example, space can be left in the tape to serve the needs of outlying divisions; or an additional program can allow for the preparation of vital statistics used irregularly but needed in a short time when a crisis arises. Putting these things in provides flexibility; leaving them out does not.

Many books have been written on business systems which will help the systems man; from them he will learn the fundamentals and the theories behind the recommended practices. But he will be wise to recognize that books do not define business needs. Every business is different, if only because different people are involved.

We may argue with idealistic fervor that individuals do not influence business needs, that it is indeed always the other way around, and that anything else would be a compromise of ideals. Though this may be true, the data processing systems man must be realistic and live with fact; he must recognize at all times that he is the bridge of understanding between the machine and the operating man over a line representing business needs. The line will not be a straight one; it will necessarily be bent here and there by compromise.

The systems man who is unwilling to compromise and who hews strictly to lofty ideals will get little done unless he bludgeons the customer with boss-said-itis. And if he does, he will learn to his sorrow what small returns are paid for being too right.

The wise systems man will recognize that the majority of his problems stem from customer unfamiliarity with the equipment and not just from the human desire to assert individual will. Whenever there is a question, he will test the water; when he finds it too hot, he will cool it with compromise. In doing so, however, he will arrange for flexibility where needed, so that at some later time he can change or adjust the thing being compromised at the moment.

The Promotion of Change

Someone has described status quo as Latin for "the shape we are in." Though this may not be a technically correct definition, it is descriptive of the state of affairs defended by the hidebound proponent of the steady boat. Even rivers sometimes change their course, but some men will always need a nudge. The use of data processing equipment has provided much of the push toward innovation in business systems, and yet evidence of resistance to change still appears in the modern system description.

Item: A company installed payroll on data processing equipment in 1940, starting with punched card equipment and progressing through successive generations of computers until today the job is done on one of the most modern high-speed machines available. The system is pointed to with pride, and the speed with which the job is accomplished defies comprehension. Yet, despite all the wondrous equipment, the methods and logic used in the performance of the job make us think of the farmer who hooked his plow to the family auto, even though a mule could have done the job better. This company, like many others, is a victim of the "Chinese copy"—a system whereby things are done in the same old way but with a different set of machine covers.

The files being kept by the payroll department are the same as those used in 1939, the year before the system was installed on data processing equipment. Personnel records are hand-kept by both personnel and payroll departments, and the same man who reconciled the bank account by hand 20 years ago is still doing so in the same way. Why? Because the controller believes that personal verification of every check endorsement is necessary to protect the assets of the company. Of course, there are other safeguards which can be taken to provide good internal control, but this man will not change. He needs a push, but who is to supply it?

When top executives are so unswerving in adherence to the old methods, who can be expected to promote change? Not many; and those who do want change are likely to change jobs in desperation.

In many companies without policy statements, systems work is carried on under the shadow of musty tradition and compromise. Compromise is desirable in dealing with systems detail, but compromise of progress is not. Data processing systems are today filled with compromises of progress, and management is seldom free of fault. When a manager vetoes changing some procedure, he establishes restraints around which the systems man must maneuver as he goes about designing his system.

These costly compromises in systems design occur as often in the modern electronic data processing systems as they do in the hand systems which furnish the input. The solution is to challenge old ideas with the same vigor with which we examine the new. And the top men should be the leaders in this endeavor.

Management Participation in Systems Design

We often hear these questions asked: Who determines the extent of the system? How do we set the parameters within which information will be generated? These are best answered by more questions: Who specifies the size of a building? Who decides the width of a highway? Who determines how long a runway should be to ac-

commodate the most aircraft? It certainly is no accident that a building is 14 stories high and contains 100,000 square feet of floor space—
it was designed that way.

There is an interesting comparison to be made between the
construction of physical and nonphysical things. Though a building is
poorly designed and sadly lacking in utility, it will nevertheless have
recognizable lines defining inner and outer limits. A data processing
system, or any other business system, should likewise be well defined;
it is as expensive as brick and mortar, or more so, and installing a
system without plans is as difficult as erecting a building without
prints.

The lack of good documentation in systems is a result not only of
the harum-scarum growth of industry, but also of the fad of decentralization. Decentralization and divisionalization were brought on by de-
teriorating labor markets, by lack of room for facility expansion, and
perhaps, in a case or two, by emotional conflict in upper management
ranks. The effect has been to spread available managerial talent so
thinly it is often only a veneer. Hand in hand with the shortage in
managerial talent and divisionalization is the bugaboo of unwritten
policy or—even worse—no policy. With the home office now 2,000
miles away, we have no opportunity to ask casual questions of the
"old man" while in the washroom.

Divisionalization has on occasion led to declining profits and loss
of control. In some cases local management, out of sheer frustration,
has been known to order data processing equipment to solve control
problems which were really policy problems at the start. Without
authority and without recognition of the need to set policy at a
divisional level, the data processing equipment can become a
glamorous tool of confusion and automated waste. Divisionalization
will always add to our difficulties in the proper use of data processing
equipment unless the business needs of the division are provided
for in written policy statements.

Management sometimes spends a good deal of time in conference
on a small personnel policy matter to protect manpower inventory or
increase efficiency in the shop. Yet we would be called daft if we
proposed that the president of a large corporation or the general
manager of a division spend time defining the information required
from his data processing systems. Though the machines build in a
"fear factor," little more time is actually required to define the

needs of a machine system than of a hand system. The executive who denies the importance of his part in systems definition certainly cannot deny that the cost of data processing is greater than the monetary value of many items to which he devotes so much time. And until business needs have been defined, and systems can be tailored to meet the needs, a computer which may cost $500 an hour is "loafing on the job." Management will make better use of data processing equipment when it better understands its own needs for information. It is neither a function nor a capability of machines to determine need.

If we do persuade top management to take more interest in data processing, we must also be warned about its taking too much interest. Its principal activity should be to define output needs: for example, sales reports by salesman by weeks, labor by department and job. But beware—many executives become technically addicted. Boss-said-itis and confusion inevitably follow.

Integration Versus the Total System

The word "integrated" connotes the complete interrelation of one thing with others. Thus the rather loosely used term "integrated system" can be mistakenly understood as meaning "total system."

The total system has small chance of being achieved within its idealistic definition. The reason is that to have a total system there must first be total integration of all the procedures which furnish the fundamental operating tools of the business. Such integration is possible, but possibility and probability are words describing two different degrees of chance. The probability of consolidating management desire and business needs in one total system is so remote that calculating the odds would defy the most experienced handicapper.

The total system is seen by its proponents as one massive file on a computer which by direction of its master program becomes the brain and muscle of all information processes. All data in the system would be stored in the same file and could be secured by coding an inquiry to the master file. For instance, let us assume we want to know the sales output of salesman Joe Blow. We inquire this way: 14-00-00-00-00-01. The first figure ("1") denotes sales; the second ("4"), salesman; and the last instruction ("01") means "give the sales record." To this coding we might add the employee number of

Joe Blow; then it is fed into the computer and out comes Joe Blow's sales record. The four other codes provided by the total system (each represented by "00") give us other coded information: perhaps Joe's personnel record; a listing of his travel expense reports, showing such elements of cost as laundry; a printout of his personality profile; a list of his skills in other fields; and a statement about his hobbies.

Preposterous though it may sound, this is close to the description of a total system as it exists in the minds of some. Should we be able to design and build such a total system, the file maintenance problem and documentation job would be double nightmares. A manager might, for example, ask to split the St. Louis sales territory because "it's too big for one man now." The technician could conceivably answer, "We are out of core storage on St. Louis. Can't you split Chicago? We have plenty there." Ridiculous? Don't bet on it.

A more reasonable approach is the concept of integrated system design which uses the same computer and incorporates the same information, organized differently. Instead of one file, there may be five, and several steps will have been taken to integrate the files. Some of the considerations in coordinating systems into an integrated whole are these:

1. Each system constitutes a separate file.
2. All commonly used coding is compatible.
3. Files are put on drums, discs, or tape so that they may "talk" to each other.
4. Each file has built-in flexibility, allowing changes to be made easily.
5. The files are established functionally for maximum use without disturbing unneeded files or "passing" unnecessary information.
6. Each file can stand alone or can be used with others.

Note particularly the last point; it is probably the most important. If a file can stand alone, the system which generates it can be designed alone. This is the advantage of integrated systems over the total system. Progress and payoff are quickly attainable through intelligent integration of systems, while a total system, if it can be developed at all, will be costly, slow, and arduous to install and may defy maintenance.

*Good coding is the very foundation of good machine systems;
management should therefore review and understand the
composition of the principal coding schemes.*

10. Coding as a Tool
Of Management

WHEN WE WANT TO BUILD A HOUSE, WE USUALLY HIRE AN ARCHITECT:
He draws up a set of plans and specifications and also monitors the
work of the contractor to see that the house is constructed according
to plan.

The proponent of the total system may point to this analogy as
proof that a system should not be installed until all plans are complete and, what is more, that nothing should be done until all
procedures are developed. Superficially this may seem to be the
logical conclusion; in fact, however, his definitions of plans and
procedures are not the same as ours.

We can apply our analogy between building a house and building
a system to practical considerations: Seldom, if ever, has there been a
set of blueprints which specified where the carpenter should drive
nails or where the electrician should drill holes in the joists to run
wiring, although they may specify the size of nails and the wiring to be
used. Plans are rarely that detailed. They give measurements, indicate
where the doors should be framed, and so on. But corrections and
changes are almost certain to be made before construction is complete.
The architect is not always able to anticipate and provide for every
minute detail. And neither is the systems man.

A system is a set of plans, something to start with. To build our
house we must shoot the grades, pour the foundation and piers, and
put in joists and plates; then we subfloor. The right kind of system
approach is not so much like building one house as it is like construct-
ing houses in a tract. We may prefabricate all the window frames for
the tract in subassemblies and cut the roof rafters for later installation
where they are the same. And, when we do build subassemblies, we

81

expect to have small troubles fitting the pieces, but we nevertheless save time and money.

The same approach can be taken to a data processing system: First we outline the entire plan, not in detail but sufficiently to describe what the system will be when finished. This is our plan of the tract with the number of each model to be built. As, in building, we do our layout and grading and then pour the foundations, just so, in a material system, we code material in machine language. Solid foundations are as important to building good systems as they are to building good houses.

The *method* of coding is a policy matter; the actual *assigning* of the codes is a detail. There is good reason for this statement. Certain codes will be used in many parts of the completed system. For instance, the material codes—which we compared to the foundation of a house—will appear on purchase orders, receiving records, warehouse bins, production orders, inspection records, and myriad other operating documents. If the coding is done properly, it will enhance all related systems, hand or machine. If it is done improperly, there will be eternal chaos.

It is necessary, therefore, to put much study into the coding to be used in any system; and because of the large volume usual in a material system, this is a critical item. It is also a good example to use in discussing coding.

Significant Coding

When developing material codes, all possible uses must be explored and the need for "significant" numbers must be investigated. Significant numbers may be thought of as "name" numbers because their positions, as related to each other, show identity and description. For instance:

Code	Article
10 or 1X*	Sheets
20 or 2X	Pillow cases

* X means another number will be added.

Thus "10" is the "name" for sheets; "20," for pillow cases. Second digit coding is added as follows:

Code	Color
01 or X1	Green
02 or X2	Yellow
03 or X3	White

Now "11" is sheets, green; "21" is pillow cases, green. These are significant digits, and their importance is easily recognized in a material system where the easy identification of "family" numbers will be helpful, particularly in storing and buying. If screws are assigned major code 01, for example, every detail code number preceded by major code 01 is readily identified as a screw.

When we discuss significant digit coding, we should recognize that it has not only advantages but also disadvantages. As in all things, overindulgence will cause trouble. For instance, in our example screws are identified by family number 01, and four more digits identify each separate class in more detail.

Major Family Code	Wood or Metal	Type of Head	Brass or Steel	Type of Drive
01	1 = wood	1 = round	1 = brass	1 = slot
	2 = metal	2 = flat	2 = steel	2 = Allen
				3 = Phillips

The codes are interpreted as follows:

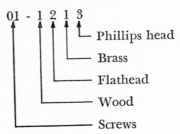

```
01 - 1 2 1 3
              └─ Phillips head
            └──── Brass
          └────── Flathead
        └──────── Wood
      └────────── Screws
```

Thus code 01-1213 describes a wood screw with a flat head, made of brass, with a Phillips drive. There may be many variations of the same screw in different sizes, so that we could go on and on adding codes for size and other specifications until we had a 20-digit code for screws alone. This would, of course, be undesirable and even ridiculous—unless we are in the business of making screws. Then we might consider such coding for programing production or for sales analysis.

Overuse of coding can cause it to lose significance simply because the users cannot remember all the digits' meanings. Conversely, too little use will minimize the ability of people and machines to recognize groupings desired for management purposes.

Sample Coding Problem

To give an example, we shall assume there is a need, in the business of selling screws, bolts, and washers, to get separate reports on family groups:

Code for Family Group
01 = screws
02 = bolts
03 = washers

When setting up the machine system, provision is made to control the family number so that totals of activity or ending inventory by products are disclosed. Also, while investigating the system, we determine that management needs to know the metal from which certain hardware is made. Heretofore, this information has been obtained through estimating techniques, but the need is now critical enough to justify the addition of coding in the system. (This is an important consideration in coding: Is it really needed?) The material manager tells us that hardware made of titanium costs so much that almost any identification procedure is justified. He states that cost is also a consideration in using stainless steel, brass, and certain other alloys.

With this information in mind, we take another look at our coding. We have assigned 01 to screws, 02 to bolts, and 03 to washers. The "0" in the first position has been provided because the company has made plans to go into two other product lines later on: hand tools and pipe. Provision for this has been made by assigning the first digit, "0," to hardware, and reserving "1" for hand tools and "2" for pipe. Thus the three product lines are 0X, 1X, and 2X. We review these preliminary coding plans and become concerned because we are sure there will be more than nine major types of hand tools and certainly more than nine major types of pipe. But we are not creating a system from scratch; the coding for hardware is already provided for the old system, which we are redesigning and incorporating in the new one.

After full investigation of the present problems we decide that more flexibility must be provided without actually changing the hardware codes. Instead, the family group coding is changed by adding a third digit. Thus:

Family Group Coding Scheme	Product Line	New Code	Old Code
0XX	Hardware	001 = screws	01
		002 = bolts	02
		003 = washers	03
1XX	Hand tools	101 = to be assigned	
		102 = to be assigned	
		103 = to be assigned	
		etc.	
2XX	Pipe	201 = to be assigned	
		202 = to be assigned	
		203 = to be assigned	
		etc.	

But we still have not solved the problem of metal identification in the hardware category. Four-digit numbers for each hardware item in each family have already been assigned, and it is easy to change the major code for the family by adding a zero in front. The problem is to identify each hardware item as to type of metal without disturbing the already established sequence according to physical configuration.

The total coding structure at this point is the same as the old one but with the zero added to the three-digit family code, as follows:

001-XXXX

The X's represent four "not significant" digits assigned to identify a particular screw; thus 001-1568 may be a No. 4 Allenhead metal screw, brass.

Our investigation now shows that present coding, including the family code change, is satisfactory and in good order. Also, 20,000 catalogues bearing the present code numbers are in customers' hands across the country; they show screws as 01-XXXX, bolts as 02-XXXX, and so on, but this presents no particular difficulty since we have only added a zero in front. Shop orders and material bins bear the old number, too; and, after weighing all the evidence, we decide that a change in the last four digits is impracticable and undesirable because it will complicate storing. So we abandon our plan to reorganize the detail item coding by metal types within the family groups.

Since the coding for type of metal is shown only for special reporting at month-end on issues, purchases, and balances—and since it is not needed as a supplement to the material code on regular reports—we make the decision to carry a two-digit (XX) code in the material master file to designate that special reporting is necessary. We therefore assign digits 01 through 10 for metal identification. To discourage the use of this code for anything other than its first purpose, we rule that it is never to be used as part of the material code. It will be used only to produce the special reports that management requires (stating type of metal or any other information that may later be wanted) and will remain a dormant code at all other times—in the master file but not in the processed detail paper.

We discover another problem while studying our coding. Although the numbers for hardware are currently in good shape, there is evidence that carelessness in the previous assignment of new numbers has created a shortage of the "in between" numbers needed for future expansion of the file. Unless some other provision is made, numbers will have to be assigned out of sequence—which means that catalogues cannot be run on the machine without first rearranging the sorting as a preliminary to listing. We solve this problem by assigning a dash number to the present code. Thus:

$$XXX\text{-}XXXX\text{-}(XX)$$

Suppose, for example, the following codes are now assigned for two screws:

Code	Name
001-1565	AN8-3
001-1566	AN9-5

A new screw (AN8-40) is added which, by size and description, must be fitted in between. It is done this way:

Code	Name
001-1565	AN8-3
001-1565-(50)	AN8-40
001-1566	AN9-5

The dash is assigned at the halfway point in our example; in actual practice it may be done more scientifically if the person assigning the numbers is knowledgeable about probable requirements and therefore able to place it precisely where it belongs in the sequence.

At this point our material coding scheme is established:

Material Code

XXX	=	family number (significant)
XXXX	=	item number
XX	=	overflow dash

Other (Dormant) Code

XX	=	in master code for special reporting purposes; not part of material code.

Although we were handicapped somewhat by the presence of a coding system already in use, we have nevertheless developed a sensible scheme which will sequence material, provide for proper machine totals, allow much flexibility, and make possible special reports on certain selected items.

In addition, of course, other codes are needed. We will want to know whether a part is "make or buy," for example, and what the unit of measure is—that is, pounds, thousands, or whatever. And there will be other dormant coding based on the requirements of the individual business.

The purpose of this rather detailed discussion of a specific coding problem has been to stress the need for serious attention by management to the establishment of coding schemes. This concern should be directed mainly toward two points: flexibility and ability to furnish desired information with maximum ease.

Controlling and Totaling

Levels of totals are secured by ascending value coding, or what we may term indenture coding. Leaving our hardware codes, let us select another subject to use as an example. Let us assume, in fact, that we have taken a census of women to determine what characteristics they prefer in men, and that we have classified our women according to age groups in our first code. (Please don't ask how we managed to learn their ages.)

Age Group	Code
18 to 23	1
23 to 28	2
28 to 33	3
33 to 40	4
40 to 45	5
45 to 55	6
55 and up	7

Now we code some of our men's most obvious characteristics:

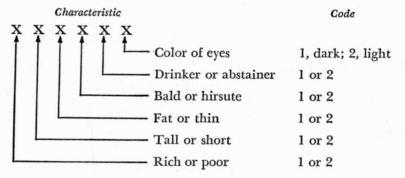

Characteristic	Code
Color of eyes	1, dark; 2, light
Drinker or abstainer	1 or 2
Bald or hirsute	1 or 2
Fat or thin	1 or 2
Tall or short	1 or 2
Rich or poor	1 or 2

When the census is complete, we can tabulate the women's age groups (coded 1 through 7) to show both individual totals at each level and cumulative totals as follows:

1	Women aged 18 to 23 who like—
1X	Rich (or poor) men
1XX	Tall (or short) men
1XXX	Fat (or thin) men
1XXXX	Bald (or hirsute) men
1XXXXX	Drinkers (or abstainers)
1XXXXXX	Men with dark (or light) eyes

In sorting we start with the seventh digit and proceed back to the first, putting our report in the order shown. Totals will be accumulated in ascending order:

Level of Totals

Women who like—

1st	Men with light (or dark) eyes
2nd	Drinkers or abstainers
3rd	Bald or hirsute men
4th	Fat or thin men
5th	Tall or short men
6th	Rich or poor men
7th	Total for age group

Then we go on to our next-oldest group of women, and so on.

When this procedure has been completed, we can select out any single group: for instance, women aged 40 to 45 who like rich men.

Use of Letters for Coding

Since a general-purpose computer is a digital machine, the use of numbers is preferable in coding. Then, too, people are trained to remember numbers—within reason. For example, it is easier to remember 1782 than XBTD.

Most often the use of letters is forced upon those who are careless about their coding plans. Suppose for a moment that originally assigned codes have two digits, 00 through 99. Suppose, further, that this group of codes proves insufficient as the number of items comes to exceed 99. To expand the coding, new items must be coded as A1, A2, and so on. Proper evaluation when the numbers were assigned initially would have avoided this problem.

Yet letters are often preferable on auto license plates, for example. A series of two letters and four numbers makes possible more than 7 million plate numbers, and this total may be expanded still further by using combinations of numbers and letters as the first two characters. The State of California uses three letters and three numeric digits to produce more than 17 million plates. The use of six numeric digits (including zeros), on the other hand, produces only 999,999 possibilities.

As a general rule, letters should be avoided in coding business problems. They create difficulties in input (alphabetic punches must be used), in sorting, and, in general, throughout all procedures. If letters are used, however, the "O" and "I" should be eliminated because they look too much like numbers.

The Question of Cross-Referencing

Telephone numbers are listed in alphabetic order by individual, not by code. Therefore, to be able to find the name of the person who has a particular number without phoning, we must use a cross-reference. The common cross-reference of the telephone directory is the street address; by using this information we can even learn what neighbor has a phone if the person we want to reach does not himself have one.

Most systems that use coding require a catalogue or cross-reference. The codes are assigned to objects and sequenced by code. The catalogue or cross-reference listing is arranged in object order and refers back to the codes.

In the material system we have used, code numbers were assigned to all material items. Since manufacturers assign numbers of their own, why not use theirs instead? This has been tried and will not work for many reasons, the main one being that any manufacturer may change his coding at will and throw the system based on vendor numbers into a quandary. Good sense therefore dictates that we establish our own system using numbers which we alone control. This is not simply another detail; it is a vital part of policy.

Vendor numbers can be used, however, as a means of cross-reference. By way of an example, we shall use four items or part numbers only, though in actuality a file may contain 40,000 items instead of four.

Our Code Number	Vendor Code or Part Number
01-1715	25635-4—screw
01-1682	A52-AB3—screw
02-2581	1216-14C—bolt
03-3375	250-B-4—washer

We can readily see the problems involved in cataloguing such disparate numbers so that an item or part can be located when we have only the vendor code. In theory, the numbers could be punched exactly as shown, and sorting from right to left should line them up. It would in fact work for the four numbers in our simple example, but what if the file did indeed contain 40,000 numbers written in every conceivable way? For instance, here are three descriptions of the item represented by code 01-1682:

Screw	A52AB3
A-52AB-3	Screw
A52-AB3	Screw

How do we cope with this problem? We set up rules for punching these numbers uniformly, regardless of how they were written originally:

1. The word description, if any, and the manufacturer's name (if needed) will always follow the part number, and a space will be skipped between the end of the part number and the name.
2. In punching part numbers:
   a. Spaces will not be put between numbers and letters.
   b. Spaces will not be put between letters and letters.
   c. Spaces will be put between numbers and numbers only where shown.

We punch our descriptions as follows:

Vendor Code (Part Number)	Our Code Number
1216 14C bolt	02-2581
250B4 washer	03-3375
25635 4 screw	01-1715
A52AB3 screw	01-1682

The order shown is arrived at by sorting from right to left. The cross-reference file is arranged so that numbers beginning with numeric digits precede those that begin with alphabetic digits. After we become accustomed to using this technique, it is quite simple. In fact, it is a necessity.

Responsibility Coding

Management sometimes appears to bypass or forget the basic philosophy that a good system establishes the responsibility of people. This is because the complexities often appear so great as to make a seemingly impossible task of it. In the use of data processing equipment we have an excellent opportunity to establish responsibility through intelligent coding. Let us therefore go a little further with our material system as a continuing example.

The buyers in our purchasing departments are assigned to specific types of material. If we give each buyer a code and put this number in our data processing master material record, we establish in that record his responsibility for each item so coded. If a buyer is handling two or three types of material, we give him two or three numbers so that, if his responsibilities are divided up later, we will not have coding problems. Now, when we make material reports by buyers, showing the condition of their inventories, we have an account of their stewardship. The finger is pointing straight at them and they know it. This is an extremely useful part of a well-coded material system.

General Remarks

It may seem that we have covered the problems of coding in entirely too much detail. Possibly so, but this is one of the areas where data processing systems break down as a result of inadequate planning or control.

In one case, the president of a company became interested in the coding scheme to be used for material. It could be said he was dealing in details. Actually he was not. He made a policy statement that code numbers were to be assigned from a central place and that codes for common parts in one division were to be the same as in another. As a result, the excess parts in one plant or division could be moved to another; proper coding provided both visibility and recognition. This president, by making a wise decision, saved his company a considerable amount of money.

A material system has been used in most of our examples on coding, but these same philosophies apply equally to others. The foundation needs to be solid, and responsibility must be established. Of particular interest to top management is the fact that data processing equipment offers the best tool for establishing responsibility since titles were invented. Titles certainly do not mean much today, but responsibility and accountability are still needed. And with good data processing techniques we can boil a lot of confusing detail down to a few pertinent facts and nail responsibility to the wall with 20-penny spikes.

11. Forms and Control

THERE IS A COMPANY WHICH HAS, AS PART OF ITS MATERIAL procedures, some 25 different forms which are used to furnish input to the computer. This is so excessive as to be laughable.

Only a few things can happen to material: It is bought, accepted or returned, used or not used; or it is shipped out and accepted or returned. Oversimplified though this list may be, there is seldom a need for 25 different forms to furnish input to one computer business system. We should be able to hold the number of material forms under ten. The basic ones might be these:

· Receiver form.
· Rejection form, designed also for OS&D as well as for use on the factory floor.
· Requisition or issue paper, designed also for returning goods to stock.
· Shipper or packing list.

These are the main input forms, and there are still a half-dozen left without having to remember that when we are returning material to stock we must use blue form 128654 for hardware or blue form 128655 for something else—except on Friday after one o'clock, the cutoff time for the week, in which case we should use blue form 128656 or green form 128657. Some of us do well to find our place of work in these times of fantastic acceleration, and we who are color-blind have difficulty telling blue from green even if we know it's Friday.

Then, on top of multiple copies and assorted colors, there are code numbers to be digested. The same company that has 25 input forms covering its material procedures has its share of codes. For instance, it lists some 15 reasons why material may be returned; 14 are coded 01 to 14, and the other—the one commonly used—is called "15–miscellaneous." Nor is this the end of the perils in this operation, for as many as 250 people may furnish unaudited input to the computer, making the chances of error in input astronomical. And added to all this is a complete lack of internal control over input and report preparation in the machine room. Result? The executive would be wise to guess rather than to use the reports that are generated.

Many times people have said, "It can't be wrong if it's keypunched and key-verified." Or, "The computer doesn't make mistakes." These are famous last words just before bankruptcy proceedings begin.

Checks and Balances

What is needed, first of all, to help solve many internal control and reliability problems is good form design. Wherever possible, when forms are filled out they should be self-coding. If blocks are provided for checking the selected item, the code for that item should appear. Also, intelligent use of mechanical data collection may relieve input problems by minimizing the number of forms required.

Recently, one of the country's leading public accounting firms expressed an opinion on the internal control aspects of using mechanical data collection equipment. The implication was that public accountants would view such a system favorably and that the accounting firm would give favorable opinions on clients' procedures if input was properly balanced to controls. Actually this was not so much an opinion as a tacit warning to be careful in the installation of data collection systems.

The truth of the matter is that even after we get information to the computer on forms or by mechanical data collection, there are still many internal control problems. The need for such control may be compared with the production and transportation of milk. If we took a bucket to a cow, milked her by hand, and then took the bucket directly to the kitchen, we could claim a high degree of internal control. We would, by visual surveillance, be careful that the cow did not switch her tail in the bucket and that foreign particles did not enter the container before, during, or after the milking operation. Since the advent of milking machines, however, more cows can be milked faster. Owing to the fact that the liquid is traveling through pipes out of our sight, we now have internal control problems. We therefore have to add safeguards such as careful flushing of the system, sterilization of vital parts of the equipment, and other precautionary measures.

In both methods, the input is the same—the cow. If the cow eats bitterweed, we get bitter milk, whether we take it by hand or machine. If the cow goes dry, we get *no* milk. The method of processing does not affect the quality of input.

The fact that information can travel into the computer by mechanical data collection and then proceed through the "pipes" without visual surveillance worries the internal control specialists. And they *should* be concerned. Here the need for proper systems planning comes to the fore again. At an early stage of planning the system should be flow-charted to establish points of control.

A common mistake can be repeated when a system does not require regular daily input. Take, for example, the handling and control of material requisitions from the time they leave the warehouse until they reach the computer room. Material is often withdrawn in several locations by means of various types of forms. For instance, there may be preplanned requisitions which allow the withdrawal of material in certain cases whereas, in others, a hand-written document signed by the foreman may be customary. Faced with these difficulties, we might throw up our hands and conclude that the only possible control is careful handling, but this is not a good answer. Instead, each warehouse should batch its paperwork every day, preferably stamping a consecutive number of requisitions in an assigned series; for, if a batch of requisitions were lost, the entire system might be thrown into chaos and serious shortages might result. In addition, a count should be kept of the number of documents being transmitted to the data processing center. If there are none for a day, a report should be sent in that shows "none."

Moreover, there are still other checks and balances which are important: totals of hours by some intelligent grouping, hash totals on uncontrolled coding, extension checks on payroll, tests of crossfooting, and other necessary procedures. To settle for anything less is to put too much trust in fate.

The Proper Perspective

The *important* internal control measure, however, is the result of a management policy statement such as this: "Controls will be set outside the machine room, and responsibility for balancing will be with the customer (user), not with the data processing organization." The data processing department does have a duty to maintain accuracy during processing, and this will of course be enhanced by centralization of responsibility for input controls.

For example, let us take a job for the payroll and information department dependent on information from several sources:

Pay status changes from the personnel department.

Tax code changes from the payroll department.

Hours and pay data, also from payroll.

Address changes from other departments or from individuals.

Input procedures might show the following picture:

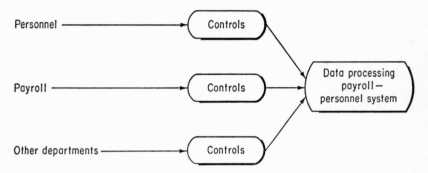

This is wrong, very wrong. Controls on one job should be localized at one point, like this:

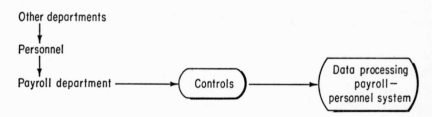

The difference:

The same thing is true for output control in the data processing department. Taking the whole cycle:

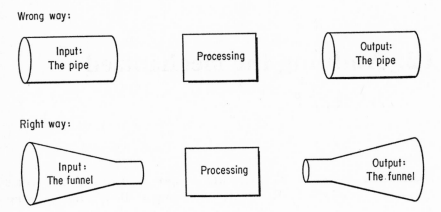

Wrong way:

Input: The pipe

Processing

Output: The pipe

Right way:

Input: The funnel

Processing

Output: The funnel

Good internal control practices for data processing are not too different from those needed in any other area of business. If we remember that the machine room is a service center which processes information from input submitted by others, we will have the proper perspective on control responsibilities.

"Auditing the computer" is not now credible, and it will be even less so in the future. Not the computer but the system which is fed into it must be the subject of the audit.

12. Auduting the Mechanized System

Recently there has been much ado about the auditor's responsibilities in an assignment involving a client's use of computers. At the one extreme in the argument are those who claim the auditor must become a programer to test records and procedures properly. At the other extreme are those who say that no checking of the computer is needed, that it is sufficient to examine the accuracy of the input and output. But most discussions become so machine-oriented that many important points are missed completely.

An article in a foremost accounting journal treated the subject of auditing a computerized client at some length, devoting considerable space to both the extremes and some of the in-between, compromise opinions. It did not adequately cover the need to make control of input data and checking of output part of the duties of an organization independent of the computer room. Yet this need is the first thing the student of auditing should recognize in studying the control of computer systems.

One of the fundamental rules of good internal control is to establish intraorganizational checks and balances. The person who receives the cash, as we all know, should not post the accounts receivable transaction. Instead, one person should receive the cash, total it, list receipts, and make the deposit. Then a list of accounts to be credited should be forwarded to another person who is independent of the cash-receiving function. Other checks and balances are applied to cash receipts, but suffice it to say that many of the traditional rules of internal control are still applicable here—and even to the uses of the modern computer.

Checking Machine Room Necessary

In considering the overall problems of computerization, we have given extraordinary emphasis to systems design. A properly designed system includes consideration of the need for auditing, with special attention to input control, balancing methods, and, eventually, proofs of balance to a point of responsibility outside the computer room. Out of necessity, however, the computer installation must also do some balancing to check the validity of output. Usually this is done in the machine room, not as a final verification of accuracy but as a check on the need for rerun. It would be foolish to complete a report without making some test of accuracy, because if a rerun is necessary, the time to do it is while the machine is set up for the job. Even if we were to question such reasoning, we would be hard-pressed to deny that balancing must take place during processing, and that unless the results of a run are checked on the spot before proceeding to another run, we cannot assure efficient operation of the equipment.

A check of accuracy in the machine room is not in itself sufficient, however, to assure good internal control. To generate acceptable controls we must first adopt the philosophy that the computer room is a service operation responsible for the processing of data but not for accuracy. This does not mean that the machine room can be operated in a relaxed atmosphere of indifference to what comes out of the machine, because the very act of processing includes many interim steps of reliability testing, spelled out by the system, without which the output would be useless.

Auditors should be well pleased to find the rules of good internal control applied in the use of computers; that is, to discover that

1. An organization outside the computer room furnishes reliable input data with adequate controls to use in balancing.
2. The computer organization balances input data before beginning the processing cycle and continues the balancing or testing of procedures at key points throughout, as specified by the system write-up.
3. An organization outside the computer room checks output to controls established outside the computer room.

Here, somewhat oversimplified, are the rudiments of good internal control from the standpoint of responsibility placement. The auditor must satisfy himself on these fundamental points before proceeding. He will find it meaningless to test machine routines of data handling unless he knows that the data being processed in the routine were reliable at least at the start. It is in checking output that he will have more difficulty, even though he has previously satisfied himself that reports are finally balanced independently to input controls. This is the point that is troubling audit specialists unduly today.

Tests of procedures within the machine room are not so sensational or so difficult as they are often said to be. Take the example of a payroll for which the auditor has already tested the input and output controls. He is satisfied that hours are balanced to the payroll department controls in the machine room and that the payroll department can verify the hours that appear on the payroll register. He is, at this point, more concerned with rate extensions, tax computations, and document counts which will insure that one employee's hours are not added to another's time, an error which will not show up in total-hours balancing. He may find that his client has established "hash" rate totals and has document-count control, both of which are carried through regular processing procedures. If so, his load is lightened; but he will still be obliged to test computations until he is satisfied that no serious defects are present in the machine system.

The auditor who goes to the machine room with the expectation of seeing and verifying figures as they whirl through the computer will be disappointed to find that the interim processing is impossible to examine. He will see people standing around the machines as the tape units silently spin their figures into the processor or accept the answers, and he will not be able to tell the difference. Occasionally, one of the operators will open a tape drive, take off a reel, and replace it with another. Now and then the console printer will type out a group of figures which he will look at and find meaningless. Then, finally, our auditor will brighten as he sees an operator preparing to write payroll checks. Now he will get a look at something he can understand—he thinks. But, when the printer starts running, the auditor sadly finds he is looking at a several-hundred-lines-a-minute blur of numbers, headings, and lines which might as well be printed in Greek so far as the value of observing the run is concerned.

In short, the auditor can do little in the machine room except to verify the necessary data control points and those safeguards described in the system definition. After satisfying himself on data handling, he may as well retire to a place far removed from the machine room.

Eventually he will find he should test the methods of the computer in the same way he would test the work of an operator who was figuring the payroll on a Comptometer. In other words, he will select samples of input—possibly time cards—and check them on the payroll register to verify that they were properly handled. He may, during his audit of the system, find that the computer has built-in checks. For example, if a man is coded on the day shift and is still drawing a night bonus, the machine will pounce on the error and print out an exception report. The auditor will not be able to see the machine do this, but he can ask for proof that it will—perhaps by looking at an instance where it has occurred or even, if he dares, by asking that it be done deliberately during processing so that he can verify the action.

Normally the auditor will be able to satisfy himself by checking the "Comptometer operator" and the system description, but he may have assignments where everything is in doubt and where procedures are described poorly, if at all. Control may be lacking, and a general state of confusion, even incompetency, may prevail. In this case, the auditor will be well advised to stand back, take a broad view of the problems, and remember that the computer is certainly not in itself the reason for such chaos. In an organization where confusion exists, the problems will still be there regardless of what equipment, if any, is being used. So, though the presence of a computer can unduly influence him to conclude otherwise, his task is not different solely because of the machine.

A good plan is to consider the machines as the means of producing the result and, in the audit program, to concentrate on machine room adherence to the system and to the policies on which the system was based.

Auditing Problems of the Future

In the spring of 1964 one of the major machine manufacturers announced a new model or, more accurately, a new machine configuration concept. The most significant difference between this machine system and others is the use of large quantities of integrated peripheral storage and communication gear. The system is also noted for its modularity, allowing rental or purchase of small to large configurations which may be increased or decreased in size by field technicians. Though modularity is not a new idea, the system is the most flexible to date in other ways.

Strangely enough, this new computer system seems to adapt an old principle to a new technology; that is, the use of special-purpose peripheral units instead of one "monster" which has been expected to do everything and has not. There is some similarity between this system and the module idea used in configuring card equipment where sorters, collators, and other pieces of equipment are separate units and can be used independently or, in some cases, together. Increments of the new system may be used in such ways, separately or together with other units, so as to eliminate a major objection to the use of a single machine—the complete tie-up of one main frame while performing minor tasks.

This new equipment, with all its advantages, will be certain to compound control problems. The reason is an interesting paradox. The equipment seems to represent the first real attempt at modern machine integration, with input, output, and all peripheral gear operating in a common language and in unison. But the concept, though certainly desirable, raises many questions, one of the biggest of which is whether man will be able to use integrated machines before he has learned to design integrated systems.

This equipment, and other machines of the future, will count heavily on random access and integrated system design to eliminate, eventually, the need for voluminous production of paper and to provide inquiry ability and "management by exception" techniques. The desirability of these features is beyond question, but some caution should precede complete exhilaration over the capability.

There are problems in the operation and control of random files, one of which auditors are even now looking on with trepidation. Updating of the random file, the enthusiasts explain, need be done only to the items involved, without spinning tape or passing the entire file through the operation. This is true, but the auditor is still obliged to question the validity of, say, an updated control total of $100,000, where it is comprised of an old balance of $97,000, less $5,000 in deletions, plus $8,000 in additions, when only those items affected are touched. Even if the change of balance is proved on the updated items, he will need to make a periodic "add up" of the entire file to satisfy his rules of good control. He will also require "test inquiries" which will allow checking of the composition of items on a sample basis.

The problems of such control may seem at first to be explained away by the provision of mechanized procedures, and it may also be convenient to conclude that an unused file will not change when it is not touched by processing. However, without going into detail about the complexities of operating random files, it is enough to say that much thought should be given to the organization of coding to avoid lack of space, overflow of records, and other filing problems.

Random file technology is a subject in itself. Improper organization of coding and filing can play havoc with the use of mechanical random access files just as it can with the use of card files in a manual system. This, of course, is not a fault in machine configuration and takes nothing away from the desirability of random capability. It only punctuates the need for studious attention in system design.

The auditor will face many more problems as machine systems become larger, more integrated, and more "real time"-oriented. He will find himself less and less able to "audit the computer" and more and more obliged to audit the system. He must therefore turn to participation in the design of the original system as a solution. Only in this way can he institute safeguards by requiring audit printouts and other check points as part of original system requirements. Inability to take part in the design of control features for the new systems will place him in the position of a protector of the assets without the means to safeguard them.

The auditor should, in the last analysis, remember this rule: Now and in the future, do not audit the computer alone; instead, audit the system and it will cover the computer.

Fixed, rigid rules should not be set for evaluating data processing equipment. Rather, management should remain flexible in its judgments and alert to the certainty of change.

13. Choosing the Equipment

ACQUIRING DATA PROCESSING EQUIPMENT IS RATHER LIKE ACQUIRING an automobile: There are many makes and models to choose from, and there is also a rent-or-buy decision to make. Most users have leaned toward leasing for these basic reasons:

- Technology has been changing too fast to consider purchase, not solely because equipment has improved but also because new ideas in systems have changed machine configuration needs.
- A manager selects the equipment he thinks is right for his needs, but he may still be fearful that production will prove him wrong—so playing it safe seems the best bet.
- Leasing is thought to place more responsibility for maintenance on the maker, and maintenance of a computer is recognized by all as a big factor; it is in fact one of the most important considerations in selection of equipment.

These reasons are not necessarily still applicable today. The rent-or-buy argument on facilities has received much mileage over the past few years and should be given still more when the question of computer utilization is considered. It is a matter of deciding how "modern" one cares to be.

If the decision is to buy, however, it should be remembered that trading off data processing equipment is not as easy as trading an automobile; and, like the automobile, the equipment deteriorates, though possibly not so fast. A worn-out or inadequate rental machine can usually be replaced, at no cost, with new or better equipment that requires less down time and gives less mechanical trouble. This fact, coupled with the assurance of continued maintenance and the further reduction of down time, could mean that leasing would even save more money in the long run than would equipment that has been purchased and fully depreciated.

Sound practice in the selection of data processing equipment includes a simple warning: If at all possible, see the equipment in actual use on some successful operation. "Test hopping" new equipment may be thrilling, but it is also perilous. Acquiring a computer is not like building a facility; it may be possible to rearrange a floor plan, but to change data processing equipment is even more chancy.

Remember to consider this question too: What happens if the equipment breaks down? Where do you go to run your Friday payroll? Unless you are ordering a complement of two machines, or there are other users of similar equipment in the area who can help in a pinch, it will be well to think long and hard about this question. Keep in mind also that the model number of the machine does not describe it in the same way that a model number describes an automobile. If you proceed on the assumption that your job can be run on another company's machine simply because both bear the same model number, you may find you have no back-up at all.

Punched card equipment presents few rent-or-buy problems as compared to a computer. This is because, paradoxically, the computer is in many ways less flexible than punched card equipment. The computer processes larger increments of the system at once— or it should—and this is exactly the capability it is acquired for. But very often, when the equipment arrives, there are wails of disappointment from the programers. "Not enough storage!" "Too few tape units!"

What do they mean?

Visualize, if you will, a wall in a post office covered with pigeonholes. That is storage. Obviously, if there are too few holes, the letter sorter cannot sort all the mail without another pass—that is, without breaking down the material into two or more groups for processing in separate operations using the same pigeonholes. This is not necessarily undesirable, because technicians usually lean toward wanting to include too much in a single pass anyway. Still, there is a problem here, especially if the basic pass required by the system cannot be made. Some operations may have to be done at one time, so it is important to establish minimum configurations. When such minimums are determined, a hasty decision to order no more than enough to meet basic needs may be the cause of some sorrow. It would be far wiser to exceed the minimum sufficiently to take care of contingencies. Moreover, if the wrong types of equipment are purchased, they may be the cause of double trouble.

The number of tape drives needed is sometimes difficult to determine. Magnetic tape can be compared to a roll of adding machine tape on which figures have been printed. If we are looking for a certain figure, we start at the top and scan down until we locate the number. The computer "passes" the tape in the same way; so, obviously, input tape should preferably be in the sequence of other records which must be matched, compared, or similarly processed. Tape cannot be used directly to make calculations, but it can be utilized for storage in cases where it is to be run through, preferably in sequence, and not used again in the routine. If information must be re-used in the same operation, then you may need to consider increasing storage. Also, you must figure how many input tape drives are needed and what output you want to record on tape. Care should be exercised in determining this minimum computation whether you lease or buy your equipment.

"On-line printing" of reports should be avoided wherever possible so that the higher-speed computer is not slowed by a printing operation. And you will no doubt prefer tape output if you use tape input. If, on the other hand, you use card input—a comparatively slow method—punching out cards or on-line printing may prove to be satisfactory. This must be weighed and determined in different circumstances by comparing computer time against output requirements. Printing jobs may be performed from tape or cards on certain types of equipment at the same time that other unrelated jobs are being processed through the computer; therefore, it is well to consider, as a general rule, that on-line printing of an "in work" computing job will not be done simultaneously. Exceptions to this rule may be made when input is voluminous and output is small; in other words, when much detail is boiled down to a few answers.

When ordering a computer, facility cost becomes very important. All machines generate some heat which must be dissipated. Is a special room with air circulation or air conditioning needed? Are sprinklers being used? If so, imagine what a ruptured pipe or breached head would do to the equipment. You will no doubt consider a CO_2 system, and they are more costly.

Tape supply requires funds too. Check this one out. How many tapes will you need? A safe rule of thumb is to double the original estimate.

The matter of outfitting a data processing program begs another most important question. What is the future of the company—expansion plans, anticipated employment levels, and other projections? Suppose, for example, a small wholesale grocery firm that plans expansion in the future finds it has present uses for data processing equipment but cannot afford a computer at this time. The management decides to rent a small, slow-speed punched card installation and wisely plans its systems so that they may be easily converted to a computer at the date of expansion. Before ordering the punched card equipment, however, the decision to lease is found to deserve some further investigation. It is determined that the keypunch equipment will still be needed when the company changes to a high-speed installation, as will the sorter. Figuring payout on such equipment results in the decision to buy all support equipment which is common to computer use.

Taking the example further, suppose the plans for expansion are subsequently abandoned. A decision must then be made about the rented equipment—should the company continue renting or buy? If, on the other hand, the company goes through with its expansion, even ahead of the time originally planned, it may utilize service bureau time until the new equipment can be installed. There is, at that juncture, another rent-or-buy decision to make. The same questions must again be asked about future plans, and the answers will again guide management in making a decision which will allow maximum flexibility.

As is apparent from this discussion, there are many routes available to the user of data processing equipment. In the case of the grocery firm, the original data processing program could have been performed wholly by a service bureau. Or the company could have used its own keypunch equipment to furnish input to the service bureau. In each case, which of these alternates may be best will be determined by management study of the problems and questions involved.

Software

Our discussion to this point has been limited to hardware. Even if the many questions to be considered in the selection of hardware are intelligently disposed of, the equipment will be useless or at best inefficient without good software support.

Software is the manufacturer's operating system instructions or program designed to give optimum utilization of the equipment; it is also the basis for the design of in-house programing systems. Although the term "software" is sometimes loosely applied to all programs, for our purposes we shall use it to mean the basic operating system provided by the manufacturer.

All of us have had experience with products which were highly touted but which were ineffective because instructions were inadequate or because we did not bother to read them carefully. We may be prone to forgo reading the tips on how to make a product operate satisfactorily, but it is doubtful that we would make the purchase if instructions were not included in the package. Care should therefore be taken to assure that adequate software is available, or will be available, to allow programing preparation before hardware is scheduled to be delivered.

New Generations

Computers have been improved tremendously in the past ten years, and the next ten are certain to bring more major improvements. Machine users have been tempted greatly by each succeeding improvement, and—fortunately for technology's sake—some have succumbed to the tantalizing advertisements. Up to the present time there has been a need for the many improvements and increased speed offered in the new models. This is not to imply that machines have now advanced to the ultimate, but they have reached the point where other constraints are present. For instance, random access equipment has now become a credible instrument, whereas heretofore it has been ponderously slow and unusable in systems requiring large-volume reference to the files. Such improvements are responsible for new processing concepts, with the change to new "system designed" equipment appearing now in the group configurations and not so much in new machine technology.

It would be foolish to predict that equipment will not change in the future, even substantially. But the changes are likely to be incremental in nature, with more modular additions to equipment possible. Therefore, it seems that this is the time to take a new and serious look at our methods of acquiring new models, as purchase and long-term-payout leasing look more favorable.

It has been predicted that the new generation of equipment which will reach the market in late 1965 or 1966 may obsolete the 20,000 or more computers now installed. We don't need to believe it; there are installations using the archaic punched card equipment which do a better job than is done by some that use the most up-to-date computer. If they are both in working order, a new and an old automobile do the same job; so also do the cheapest model and the most expensive. Indeed, an older automobile may perform better because it is run on a better quality of fuel and has a better driver. Just so, if it is given good input and intelligent systems, an older data processing machine can be as useful as a later model. We mustn't be led down the primrose path of change for its own sake; we must look at our need, the costs, and what the new machine offers in the way of new systems possibilities. But, still, we must look, for we may find, after proper study, that we cannot afford to keep our old equipment when the new configurations are available.

The next major change in computers—a prediction we make with some courage—will be in the area of storage. Present random files are still not the ultimate answer to maintaining large libraries of information. This statement may bring violent disagreement from some; nevertheless, we predict that somehow, in some way, the next major step in storage design will be back to a unit record concept which allows easy interfiling. It cannot be mechanical, nor can it be slow, as are handlers of punched cards and other unit records.

This prediction is not based on clairvoyance, nor is it an attempt to claim unusual perceptive powers. Instead, it is based on the simple fact that unit records present fewer filing problems than bulk storage. For this reason alone, high-speed unit records of some sort will be developed.

Computer "togetherness" at its worst is better than "apartness" at its best. Not in separate installations and separate personnel and separate problems but in a unified business and scientific computing installation are the money-saving opportunities to be found.

14. Scientific Computing

AT THE END OF 1964 COMPUTERS HAD BEEN USED IN INDUSTRY FOR only 15 years, the first five of which were not overly productive and were characterized by experimentation rather than by real accomplishment.

The many machines offered during the decade from 1955 to 1964 were classified generally in two broad categories, scientific and business, and were configured toward separateness. This was convenient for management decision making, since the widely accepted separation of business and scientific computing offered a means of avoiding a head-on collision with a new world of problems.

It was apathy that led to the widespread acceptance of separateness; and it is apathy that has, for most users, created a larger problem. Now, millions of dollars later, management faces the same need for decision; only this time it may be double-barreled—to do what is best and undo what is not.

Constraints of the Past

The selection of equipment for use in scientific applications, based on yesterday's ground rules, was almost routine. First, need was established by scientists and engineers with little or no review at the top even if top-level managers were professionally capable of intelligent evaluation. The second step was to choose between the two types of machines: (1) binary or (2) binary coded decimal. These terms describe the organization of the magnetic core and the coding of characters; beyond this let us simplify our discussion by giving the edge in speed to the binary equipment. Because of its speed, the binary mode was preferred for scientific calculations.

One of the main reasons for business preference of the binary coded decimal machine as opposed to the straight binary was the increased reliability of the bit parity check in the binary coded decimal scheme. In the more reliable modern equipment this does not appear to be a critical problem. If the reader wants to investigate details beyond the scope of this book, we suggest that he contact a manufacturer for full clarification.

Step three involved the fateful question: Is it economically feasible? Or: Can we afford it? This was answered by the application of various levels of convenient rationalization: plenty of money and business to go ahead, or not entirely feasible economically but the scientists insist, or not at all practical from a fiscal standpoint but competition demands it. Some managements—fortunately for their companies—decided computerization was economically unsound unless the machine was to be used for both business and scientific work. This stand better prepared them for the future.

Solving the Problems of Separateness

For those who have succumbed to separateness there is trouble ahead. The president of today's corporation no longer will sit still for a 19th hole dissertation on the marvels of scientific computation. His eyes are open wide now to the rush of dollars through the cash flow pipes. He knows, too, that as others solve the problem of separateness, the competitive pressure will build up.

Of course, decisions to separate scientific and business computer installations were not necessarily wrong at the time they were made. Where sufficient load was present in both areas, the decision to acquire different machines was a credible approach. And, if the workload is expected to continue, perhaps it may remain so. But even if this decision was sensible at the time, and is still sensible today, it is almost certain to be wrong in the future, and regardless of load.

Many companies that installed separate business and scientific machines assumed that separate machines suggested the need for separate organizations. In fact, however, separate organizations, by the mere weight of their duplicative functions, increase the costs of computer operation. This is quite obvious; and, in addition, there are other increases in costs which are not so obvious. The faster scientific machine will usually be equipped with a larger memory.

Some parts of the business system may utilize this capability quite well, thus optimizing load and reducing total expense. Suppose, for example, that a company has two machines, each with its own organization. If a voluminous sort for a business application is run on the scientific machine, it relieves the overload on the business machine, at the same time performing the sort at less cost. Thus a digital computer, whether commonly defined as a business or a scientific machine, may be used for either type of problem. For instance, a market analysis, normally defined as a business problem, can be programed for either machine with the same results. On the other hand, such engineering administrative problems as man-loading may be better suited for the business machine. If the installations were combined under one operating head, the problem of determining what work should be performed by which group would be eliminated.

Other advantages of merging computer operations are equally promising. Peripheral gear, the smaller supporting computers and printers, may be better scheduled for optimum use to prevent adding equipment otherwise needed for separate organizations. Supplies may be standardized and ordered in greater quantities to produce savings. Best of all, by merging operations the most talented people can be put in charge—there is the greatest payoff.

We see a new day coming very soon when the computer will no longer be classified according to its use. It will be just a computer, comfortably suitable for either business or scientific work. Then merged operations will certainly be a "must."

Problems of the Smaller Business

For many smaller businesses, a discussion of merger is completely inapplicable. Their concern centers around these questions: Do we need a computer for scientific work? Do we have a mixture of business and scientific work? If the answers are in the affirmative, and a decision is made to procure a computer, the question will then be: Should we be influenced most by business or scientific needs? There are many companies which successfully employ one or more computers of either type in both business and scientific work. The amount of money available in each case was probably a more pertinent consideration than the type of machine.

What kind of scientific problems need to be solved on a computer? This question is a difficult one for business management to deal with. The way in which it is handled will have a profound effect on the level of dollar outlay.

Even after full evaluation, management may be disappointed to find that no cost reductions are indicated. The engineers may claim—and rightly so in many cases—that the main advantages are more answers to examine for better and faster decisions. Whatever our doubts, we may have to rely on their judgment. Fortunately or not, most of the time it is this rather artless approach which is used to establish the level of need for scientific computations.

Since it is impossible to describe the details involved in the application of management judgment to evaluating this question of need, we shall assume that the matter is being pushed insistently by the engineers—or others—and that, somewhere up the line, management has decided to continue to give attention to the possibilities.

At this point we shall also assume that we have answered the question of both scientific and business need, individually and collectively —with particular emphasis on the word "collectively." This is important, for the claims of the engineer or scientist that a bigger machine or machine configuration is required will not usually be heeded if he is the only potential user and his workload is small. Suppose, however, that the business people can economically use the remaining 60 or 70 per cent of the same machine's capacity. This will at least indicate the desirability of continued investigation.

In the interest of good fiscal practice we should then take a better look at the complexity of the scientific problems to be solved on the bigger machine. Do the engineers claim that some of their calculations are too complex for a smaller business machine configuration? Caution is called for on this point. Many problems can be solved on medium-size machines by resorting to multiple passes—that is, by running a problem in sections so as to stay within machine limits. If scientific problems make up only a small percentage of the expected load, management may order a small machine configuration and farm out routines which it cannot handle. However, if the projected workload is heavy on the scientific side and speed is a prime consideration, it would probably be well to go to a larger configuration unless it is found that the workload consists of relatively simple calculations which look complicated solely because of volume. If this is true, speed should perhaps be sacrificed for the sake of lower total cost—always remembering that most scientific problems can be solved on a smaller machine.

When making studies of computers for use in business or scientific work, it will also be well to watch the input and output devices to avoid spending money putting information in or taking it out faster than the internal speed of the computer can handle it.

As is apparent by now, there are no pat answers to questions about machines for scientific computing. There is one thing, though, that will almost always be true. The really big, complex problems will usually be in the minority; so too much emphasis should not be placed on these. Unless this precaution is taken, we may be dismayed to find that only a small portion of the problems are big enough to warrant the size of the machine selected. If there are only a few difficult jobs, we can rent the time to do them. Many users are willing to sell time; indeed some are actively in the business as a sideline because they are oversupplied with power and time.

Scientific Operation: Open Versus Closed Shop

Questions arise, also, with regard to the use of the "open" and "closed" shop method of operation. In an open shop the scientific personnel do their own programing, whereas in a closed shop they state their problem and the computing department employees do the programing. We are not inclined to state a preference; however, in using the open shop method it will be wise to provide controls for checking the jobs done, lest someone surreptitiously program a routine to beat the ponies or the stock market. (This has actually happened!) Another control that should be established is a method of cataloguing routines at a central point to avoid the duplication that an uncontrolled open shop produces.

More on Organization

To repeat: Both business and scientific computing work can be combined under one department head. Machine usage—loading, scheduling, monitoring, and control—needs consolidated attention, especially if one machine services both areas. The modular equipment of the future will make this an increasingly important consideration.

Good people are harder to find than good equipment. So far as using the machine for scientific computing is concerned, it can safely be wagered that results will be no better than the people overseeing. This is true because, in solving scientific problems, every-day business requirements do not enter in; the machine may be asked to compute information on products to be manufactured five years from now. Furthermore, a business executive who is accustomed to exercising a great amount of control over the way a material system operates may find himself woefully inadequate to the task of evaluating scientific projects. As a result, he must be careful to staff the computing function, both in and out of the machine room, with the most reliable personnel available. Only then will he have the slightest chance of getting his money's worth from the equipment.

Data processing has opened up to industry a whole new world of personnel problems. To handle these problems, a special kind of management finesse is needed.

15. Data Processing Personnel Problems

THE EXCESSIVE COST OF R&D, AND THE EXCESSIVE TIME IT REQUIRES, act as safety valves on our economy; they make it impractical to invent things all over again. When we buy a new automobile, we may question the ancestry of the designer if the parts and pieces disintegrate. And, when the need arises for a replacement, we may think a design of our own making would be far superior. But the pressure of time and the problem of funding make this impractical as a do-it-yourself project. So, again, we succumb and purchase a popular make on the current market.

Of all human characteristics, the desire to create has been a principal contributor to the development of our country. There are men among us who believe everything can be done better. The fact that they continue to feel this way is more important than that they attempt and fail. Three cheers for this drive! Let us hope, despite the trend toward conforming collectivism, we continue to turn out a few of this hardy breed of doers or triers, the kind who will put their jobs on the line every day.

What has this to do with data processing? Nowhere is there a hardier breed of doers and triers than in the data processing world. One reason for this must be that the computer is relatively new and interest in the field has been heightened by its need for inventiveness.

We should not inhibit this desire for individualism; but, at the same time, neither should we allow our people to "invent" us out of business. Though we subscribe to the theory that everything can be done better, and indeed endorse it, our aim in the data processing world should ultimately be to get a job done.

It is not the intent of this book to tout any one brand of machine; nevertheless, it must be mentioned that one manufacturer in particular has been very helpful in bringing users of its equipment together into valuable organizations dedicated to the creation and dissemination of ideas. These groups meet regularly to discuss problems, methods, and organization. Official releases of their activities are published for on-the-spot use and for cataloguing back home as reference material. It is strongly recommended that top data processing personnel seek membership and officership in such groups.

Pride of authorship should never be discouraged. Rather, management should foster it in data processing people by insisting that they participate in such organizations for three very good reasons: to increase their confidence; to let them give voice to their authorship in an organization where an idea can be presented even though it may not be useful in their own shop; and to allow them to learn about (and use) ideas others have developed, including "canned" programs. By taking part in such activities the technician can find a satisfying outlet for his energies.

Personality Problems

One subject we must discuss, however touchy it may be. Data processing technicians are extremely sensitive people, and at present they can afford to be. This sensitivity is too widespread to be dismissed as congenital. It develops gradually in direct proportion to time, drive, and ability. Because the man with ten years of good experience will be much better qualified than the man who has had one year of experience ten times, sensitivity might be measured by a formula of ability to the power of time. The data processing man can afford to be sensitive, and remain so, because the business world is clamoring for his services. It is probably true that proportionately more moves are made by this group than by any other, including engineers and scientists.

Managers may equate the exodus of data processing people with a desire for more money. This may be true in isolated cases, and it may also be an irrefutable fact that when moves are made, pay increases. But the decision to make a change often stems from factors that are more complex.

The nature of the work performed by the data processing specialist creates frustrations occasioned by few other jobs. He is forever fighting deadlines in his product delivery, while at the same time coaxing a mechanical monster to do his will. If he does not meet a schedule, his pride is wounded because of his failure to tame the tangle of transistors. Woe be to the manager who heaps the fuel of criticism on top of this already roaring fire. We may claim this is true of all people—and to a degree it is—but close contact with the data processing group may prove the problems to be extraordinarily critical.

Another point to recognize when dealing with the data processing expert is that he is indeed an expert in his field. Nobody offends the technician more deeply than the man who attempts to tell him how he should program a job on the computer after attending a three-day school. Such self-styled authorities cut the technician to the quick with the apparent presumption that his job is an easy one.

Consultants: Good and Bad

There are some unreliable consulting people who are collecting large fees for unpracticed "studies" of their clients' data processing programs. An effective way to demoralize data processing people is to hire a consultant they cannot respect.

In one actual situation, preliminary talks were held with a consultant who was being considered to survey a large data processing program. The company was in need of help, but management wisely decided that some kinds of help are worse than none at all. This particular consultant, it was discovered, was by no means qualified to evaluate a data processing program; he had had no practical experience whatsoever. And to set an inexperienced theorist loose in the midst of a data processing group is a sad mistake indeed.

If a company does need to consider outside assistance—and many do—it should not trade trouble of one kind for tribulation of another. Instead, it should choose a well-qualified, knowledgeable consultant or firm and be sure the consulting role is definite and well defined before work begins.

The Data Processing Manager

We have been discussing data processing people in general; what about the top man? One of the main threats to the data processing manager is stagnation. He walks into the office one morning and suddenly realizes he has been sitting in the same chair too long. An analysis of the promotion prospects in his company shows all too clearly that the chief accountant always becomes the next controller, the manufacturing manager is heir apparent to the vice president for operations, and so on down the line. This man asks himself why management is passing him by in awarding the bigger jobs. Some of his own top people are capable of moving up to his job, and unhappily he knows they are wondering if something is wrong with him that denies them promotion.

The data processing manager has gone to the top in his field, and now he has nowhere to look but down. He has two alternatives: He can get a better-paying job outside the company which will at least give him new if not more interesting problems to solve, or he can sit and mildew.

Why isn't the data processing manager considered good material for the next job up? Possibly he has become so engrossed in details that he is not cognizant of the overall business problems. Possibly he is locked out of staff meetings because he is considered a glamorous technician who should not be bothered with the mundane cares of business at the top, even though he will hear about some of the problems later anyway, at third or fourth hand.

His boss may look at him in yet another way—with apprehension. He recognizes the value of a good man in the data processing job; it is running smoothly, and he does not want to rock the boat. It's a shame, but this is standard practice. A successful data processing manager is usually a highly developed logical thinker who could be more useful in running the business. If he were not, he would never have made the grade in his field—he would be the wrong man for his job.

Don't be surprised, on checking, to find such a man resigned to his fate and in the process of losing his zest for the day-to-day job. Alternatively, he may be concentrating furiously on his own little empire to the exclusion of the rest of the company and becoming more and more difficult to work with. He may have given up on his chances for advancement so completely that he is operating by instinct instead of reason. What he needs may be encouragement, a soothing hand, or a boot in the posterior, according to your evaluation and prescription. But, if he is a good man, get him on the job one way or another!

An excellent way to accomplish this is to invite the data processing manager to attend management meetings on other subjects. Let him hear about the business's problems and take part in the discussions. Once he understands the overall situation, you may get some of your best suggestions from him. Most important, his work may take on a new luster which will discourage stagnation. The data processing man will then be a part of management, as he should be.

Training Data Processing People

Training of data processing personnel is another subject that needs management attention—that is, the quantity and quality of instruction which will be given to the various data systems groups in or outside the data processing department.

Machine manufacturers offer training courses for technicians; and, given enough money, patience, and honest desire to build up data processing capability, management can cope with the technical training problem. However, training is a facet of the mechanizing program which is usually overdone or undercooked. The much-misquoted old saw, "A little knowledge is a dangerous thing," provides some managements with a convenient excuse for giving no training at all. Others take the view that every member of the systems team must be a technician and proceed to cram their people with useless knowledge. Both approaches are in error.

A training program which makes technicians of everyone engaged in the field will take too much time and will defeat its own purpose. Such training may create the desire in some of the group to work with the equipment instead of designing the input and output of the system, even though this is the area in which they are best qualified and in which they will be of most value to the program.

No training at all, on the other hand, leaves the systems man with the feeling that he is dealing with an incomprehensible monster. It creates fear, distrust, and a feeling of inferiority in him when he must work daily with the technician—who may aggravate matters, good-humoredly or otherwise, by applying the "needle" to the systems man for his ineptness. We must try, in short, to find a middle ground.

An excellent approach is to plan a two-and-a-half-week training program. During the first week, we might acquaint the systems man with the general uses of the equipment, explaining in lay terms the names and basic functions of the various units. Then, in the classroom, we would give him such basics as card layouts and their similarity to tape records, the nature of storage, the elements of programing—in other words, a smattering of data processing lore with all its exotic flavor.

The first four days of the second week could be devoted to going over the details of a small program, complete with instructions in simple language. Friday could then be spent back in the machine room, with the "student" actually running through the machine system covered in the sample. Finally, another two or three days might be allowed for review, the answering of questions, and perhaps a written test. Then—on-the-job training.

In actual practice, this type of approach has successfully developed a vigorous interest in machine capability without creating in all data processing people the desire to become technicians.

Management will do well to make data processing systems and the computer a part of its daily life. If it does not, it may cut its profits on the sharp edge of change.

16. Machine Decisions

IF WE HAD MODEL X111 INSTEAD OF MODEL X110, WE COULD SAVE $2,500 a month." When statements like this are made and we fail to listen, we may be accused of avoiding our fiscal responsibility. And we will be guilty.

The object of using equipment is to save money. But how can management be sure that all the relevant facts have been considered before it makes the decision to update or order new equipment? Among the questions that should be answered are these:

1. What are the actual costs of present equipment if it was purchased?
   a. Is present equipment being depreciated on an accelerated basis which inflates its cost and thereby increases calculated savings on the new machine?
   b. Is that equipment near the end of the depreciation period, hence almost at the point of being "free"?
   c. Have maintenance and other costs been added in for both present and proposed equipment? In the case of the old equipment, have they been estimated high enough to cover future periods included in the study?
2. What are the fringe costs of the proposed equipment? Are they accounted for in the estimate? This category will include additional supplies, operators, added facilities, and similar items.
3. What will it cost to develop the new equipment? Consider reprograming, training, any necessary system revision, and lap-over rental or depreciation.
4. Will the proposed new machine save so much time that it will reduce usage below a basic shift? If so, it could still be desirable. New jobs still in the planning stage can be added to the old load to produce optimum usage.

5. If the computer is used for scientific problems, will the new equipment enhance engineering capability in terms of the size and complexity of the problems which can be solved? If not, we might well question the value of increased speed—unless, of course, overload is the impelling reason for the change. Even then, we should investigate the reasons why anticipated overflow work cannot be farmed out, especially if the load problem is likely to be a spasmodic, peak-and-valley thing.

6. If the new machine offers simultaneous input-output, parallel processing, time sharing, or some other improvement, can we use this increased capability properly? We should review our systems and reprograming plans very carefully.

7. Will conversion to the new equipment require that a simulator program, or conversion package, be used? If so, for how long? Are programers available to staff the changeover so that the simulator method will not be used permanently on voluminous, repetitive jobs? If a simulator is used in an attempt to emulate the old machine processes, the new equipment may be operating far below full horsepower; actually, it could be no better than the old machine with an expensive new set of covers. On the other hand, we may rightly insist that little-used programs, and any scheduled early procedural revamping, be kept on simulation.

Still other questions will come to mind. The point is that before we order a bigger and faster piece of equipment, we want to be sure that it will pay out. If we can satisfy ourselves by ferreting out the facts, we will save money whether or not we order new equipment; and the correct decision will have been reached.

Machine Decisions of the Future

Life is not easy for the man who must make decisions about data processing equipment. However, there is some relief in sight, and it will come in a strange way.

We have already discussed some of the audit problems that will accompany future integrated machine systems. But there will also be some hidden blessings to be enjoyed in the new systems—if not for the auditor, at least for the executive in charge of data processing.

The original decision to acquire the integrated machine system cannot be made on the veranda of the country club. Neither is it likely to be the result of haranguing from the technician, who will have developed a profound respect for the problems of programing an integrated machine system. As a matter of fact, the systems and programing people may have to be prodded toward the new concept in machine systems. The reason for this anticipated reluctance will be fear, and if the technician is not afraid, be careful—he doesn't understand the problems.

What *are* these problems? The integrated machine system will be modular in configuration, true, but it will also be modular in systems application. The company that uses the integrated systems approach will gradually add jobs to the computer until, for example, it may have an innocent-looking array such as this:

1. Accounting, including payroll.
2. Manufacturing control.
3. Material control.
4. Quality control.
5. Marketing analysis.

What is different here? The files for these jobs will be contained in random access devices, discs perhaps, that can be worked against each other for related information. Input to the files will utilize data-collection methods inside the plant and microwave or teleprocessing from outside the plant. Most reports will be made only on an exception basis—for instance, the purchasing department will immediately be furnished a list of material which has reached the re-order point, or the machine may even write the purchase order automatically.

While the machine is processing these integrated systems, it will also be switching messages between plants. For example, shortly after the president receives a report on the poor performance of the sales office in Back Wash, Louisiana, he may want to send a message through the same computer firing the sales manager. This will logically be followed by instructions to the machine to prepare a final paycheck. Thus the man is quickly drummed out of the corps by electronic means.

This example may be a bit farfetched, but it indicates how complicated, though desirable, the integrated machine system will be.

A comparison may be drawn between the integrated modular machine system and "big government." Government is highly modular, with new agencies and commissions being added frequently. Although the word "modularity" implies the possibility of removal as well as addition, big government seldom does away with anything —except tax money. When systems people and programers do conquer the integrated machine system, don't expect them to do any subtracting; like the computer, they will perform all their calculations by addition.

As suggested earlier, however, once management decides to install an integrated machine system, all its later decisions will be simplified somewhat by diminution in size, and for the most part they will concern modules to be added. Perhaps we can reap some satisfaction from the fact that systems may become so efficient—and so complicated—that no one will *dare* to change them.

The Paradox of Bigness

Managers should not be frightened by machine integration, which is desirable with matching systems. However, problems will be created by bigness in computers as in almost everything else.

Suppose that five small systems are installed on the machine and integrated by use of random files and so on. They will then become one big system in the collective sense. They will require, of course, that pieces of the machine be reserved to process them. Furthermore, since they will remain in the brain of the machine, they may restrict its use for other purposes.

Thus, even with full and efficient integration of big machines and systems, it is certain there will be a need for a small computer capability to handle special jobs. Possibly this will be part of the bigger machine system, but it will still have been added for the specific purpose of handling special or small jobs.

Though improved time-sharing capability will soon be available to minimize these problems, its use must be carefully monitored. Uncensored, it will add immeasurably to the confusion and compound the problems of using the computer for its real purpose—to increase profits. System integration and time sharing are, in fact, fire-breathing dragons which must be sought out and conquered. If not, consternation will prevail.

Until all these problems are solved, we may continue to ask whether machine integration and permanent systems storage in the computer are desirable. The answer must be determined by individual soul searching; but as with the Roman Empire, bigness alone will still not suffice.

Information Retrieval

Information retrieval, or "data retrieval," is a term used to describe the method or act of data filing and recall. It connotes the use of information that is not needed in everyday processing, in contrast to a payroll or material master file which is referred to on a daily basis. An example would be a magnetic storage device holding a library of court cases. These data would be retrieved only as required.

Information retrieval is not strictly concerned with machine methods. It can quickly become a philosophical topic.

Man has always been subject to varying degrees of regimentation. Aside from those constraints which are of God's making, such as sun, moon, and weather patterns, there are some which man himself has created. Man is sensitive to time and has invented ways to recognize its passing—in his language ("Meet me in an hour"), in his machines (the clock), in his transportation systems (which run on time schedules), and in many other facets of his life.

Now the worst has happened. In addition to the more commonplace machines which goad us to daily encounters with time, we now have created a new one—the computer—which will prod us by follow-up action and error detection if we don't perform according to the rules of speed and accuracy. And, oddly enough, we gave the machine this capability by programing its "brain" to simulate our intellect. It is our own fault.

Since man loves to converse with others and enjoys the thought of posterity, he has found new uses for the computer. In addition to the more mundane applications of data retrieval equipment— master payroll files, material price histories, and the like—such things as quotations from great statesmen and whole libraries of reading material have been programed into machines, as have decision tables and mathematical models based on past criteria.

We can look forward to the time when government, faced with a problem of foreign relations, not only may get its answer from a decision table but may verify its accuracy by passing the mathematical model over the matter. It may also call on the computer to conjure up pithy, profound statements for public consumption.

Further reflection in this vein can lead us to some wide-eyed conclusions. If we can record the wisdom of our generation in the memory of a computer, will there be any need for schools? Why should our youngsters of the future be sent on a duplicative search for knowledge, other than reading and writing, when the pressure of one pudgy little finger can open up a world of accumulated knowledge?

This is facetious nonsense, of course. But, seriously, we are collecting in the meager computer memory now available much worthless information for indiscriminate dissemination. Worst of all, this information is going to people who may ascribe value to it and put it to use. To combat this problem, there has been suggested to one of the major machine manufacturers an "information disposal" system which would permit input by the "historian," give him a copy which he could retain, and then spew the words irretrievably at the speed of light into space—never again to be a threat to coming generations.

We should definitely be concerned over the possibility of cluttering our children's minds with preconceived notions of wisdom and knowledge. Nevertheless, let us not overlook the *desirable* uses of information retrieval. Sensible application of the computer to data retrieval opens up many opportunities to both business and science.

Opportunities in Machine and System Integration

The engineering department in most companies also serves a record-keeping function. Engineering costs must be estimated, budgeted, and measured against actual expenditures. The problems encountered in such an operation are complex, usually requiring special treatment. It is often important, especially in the management of R&D projects, to furnish rapid feedback so as to allocate manpower in a manner compatible with appropriations.

Data processing specialists have long labored to take over the record-keeping function of engineering. And management has endorsed it by the time-worn statement, "Let's make engineers of our engineers, instead of bookkeepers." Armed with such feeble profundities and sometimes little else, the systems people set out to "get their foot in the door." Meetings are held to determine what the engineer wants in the way of control tools. Needs are not considered, even if the systems men know what they are, and the reporting system that results is a carbon copy of antiquated, hand-kept records except for one thing—more detail.

Reports start rolling from the high-speed printers. Friday afternoon they are delivered to the administrative section of the engineering department. Which Friday? The one after the week for which the report was made. High speed indeed! The hand system must still function because the printed reports are so late they are as valuable as yesterday's newspaper. The report is used, but only to check its accuracy against the hand-kept report which was finished three days earlier and has already served other purposes. The machine report does have one other use—to prepare adjustments to the accounting records, again based on what the manual records show. Which is right? It matters little, for all management's actions in the interim have been determined from the hand records.

The engineering department is not alone in duplicating the record-keeping function. Similar excesses occur in the material function, in manufacturing areas, in the personnel department, and, indeed, in the executive's shop where the data processing function resides.

Why this duplication? Whatever the reasons, we hear the now-familiar management complaint: "We installed data processing equipment, but nobody goes out the door—we still have the same number of clerks as before." At this point, even though the proper emphasis has been given to the determination of business needs, even though the proper systems approach has been taken, another ingredient is necessary—timeliness. The speculator in the stock market cares little what an issue did a year ago except for purposes of analyzing trends. Likewise, the management engineer couldn't care less about a data processing report which tells him what he already knows. The buyer in the material department will not be impressed or helped by a report which shows a receipt to the warehouse when, in the interim, he has been obliged to order replacements for the same parts because of rejection on the floor of the factory.

Many devices are now available, some are being developed, and others will be developed which will eliminate the long wait between an event and the report on it. But we must understand that not all the reasons for failure to react to management responsibilities may be blamed on the mere passage of time in the computer room.

The attentive manager may look to random or direct access processing, data collection, and electronic inquiry for answers to many of the questions of profit deterioration due to the high costs of paper-work. All the same, he will not fail to consider business needs in terms of cost trade-offs between time and computer cost. Perhaps he will find a continuing need for some hand-kept records in the engineering department where, regardless of claims to the contrary, the group engineer who has only 15 men reporting to him can keep his records for the week on the back of an old envelope. If such is the case, a weekly report which comes out on the Friday following the close of the week is timely enough. The manager can demand, in such a case, that the engineering department limit its record keeping to simple head-count loading records, depending solely on the data processing reports for accumulative purposes.

Any consideration of the duplication problem is bound to end with the realization that management must spend more of its own time in investigation and less in discussion of the subject. Perhaps the problem can be solved very simply—cut out the duplication by dictum. If data processing equipment is being used to produce information for management, then management must insist that the information be useful and timely—but never duplicated.

17. The Future of Data Processing

Many BELIEVE THAT DATA PROCESSING EQUIPMENT HAS REACHED THE apex of its development. One government agency has gone so far as to recommend that computers be purchased and stocked by a central group, to be issued to agencies and defense contractors according to their varying needs. With complete disregard for programing and systems problems, the agency claims this procedure would save the government much money by reducing waste in the needless acquisition of new models. Also according to this agency— at least by implication—computers have reached their maximum limits of design, and the time is therefore right for purchasing equipment instead of leasing it. Studies have been made to show that the purchase of equipment four or five years back would have saved millions of the taxpayers' dollars.

No sensible person would claim that computers have been properly utilized or that the observations of hindsight do not indicate that savings would have been possible if things had been done differently. However, the experience of the past, costly though it was, must be weighed against the technological advances that have been made partly because of such waste. The same argument for frugality could be applied to aircraft: If we had frozen the Ford Tri-motor design and continued to use that model of aircraft over the years, we would have saved billions of dollars. In point of fact, the Ford Tri-motor probably is comparable in aircraft development to our present levels of advancement in computer design.

At first glance, such a comparison may seem laughable, especially to those who are in the business of designing and selling computers. It must be remembered, however, that computers are still in their adolescence. Certainly we who have seen so many wonders created in our time cannot doubt that we are only at the threshold in the development of such electronic devices.

130

New Needs—New Improvements

The reason for invention or improvement in existing technology is recognition of a need. Therefore, the advancement of computers and succeeding improvements will be sustained by newly discovered uses. For instance, within a few years we will be able to dial a friend's phone number and, if we find it busy, instruct the computer at the phone company's switching center to notify us when the phone is free. When the lines are free, both phones will ring. There may even be a special ring for us to indicate that our original request is being answered. Also, often-used numbers may be coded so that not all the numbers in a set need be dialed.

In another business, an airline company is now using computers in its highly developed reservation system. In one case, a man making a reservation for himself and his wife casually remarked that the flight to San Francisco would be made on his wife's birthday. An alert reservation clerk put this information into the computer memory for data retrieval, and the woman was presented with a birthday cake along with her lunch in flight. Result: a satisfied customer—forever.

As these examples demonstrate, computer logic can increase sales. Present models are not designed to serve all such purposes conveniently, but—for the airline company, certainly—innovation with available equipment is paying off in increased earnings. New machines better suited for communications are now being produced and will soon be marketed widely. They will offer many opportunities to those who seek to develop special adaptations for their businesses, particularly where public service is the product.

In the future, computers will find general acceptance, in engineering design, for preparing drawings—particularly electronic wiring schematics. This may be viewed with trepidation by the engineer as a threat of automation in his profession. In most cases, however, he will find the machine only relieving him of the laborious task of recording his thoughts on paper. He will be able to make a rough sketch of his plan, then let the computer take over to make the print and do the checking for design error. This capability will be especially useful in electronic design where the output of one module may be tested against the input needs of another.

Teaching is already being done by computers, and, though the method is quite impersonal, it has been proved that generally the computer-taught student of specialized subjects achieves a grade average and learning speed far exceeding those of students taught by orthodox methods. Like it or not, because of the shortage of teachers, the tutors of the future may have to learn to program courses of instruction into a computer.

Doctors will increase their dependence on the computer. It is not inconceivable that "real time" operations will be performed on the machine at the same time the surgeon is operating on his patient, with the machine monitoring respiration, heartbeat, and other essential information and printing out immediately on a screen what action the attending nurses need to take. This will free the doctor to concentrate on the job to be done within the critical time span so important in major surgery. Computers will be used to diagnose many diseases and even to arrive at methods of treating nervous disorders by searching for similar symptoms in case histories—without divulging the sources of the histories. They are now being used to search for aftereffects of drugs and dangerous combinations of medications.

Machines will certainly sort most of our mail in the future. Special envelopes will be used for all mailing, and addresses will be either printed by hand or typed in specified locations on the envelopes. Character recognition devices will then sort the mail and direct it to the proper destination. They will probably recognize air mail by the magnetic ink which will be used to print the stamps, thus directing the mode of transportation as well.

Blueprints and public records will be on video tape with voice channel. As a result, records may be easily sought out, displayed, described, and reproduced in a matter of minutes or seconds.

Many processing plants such as oil refineries are now run by special-purpose computers. Their application has been simplified somewhat by the repetitive operations inherent in such installations. But the special-purpose computer of the future will care little whether the operation is repetitive; it will have sufficient brain-power or storage so that we will be able to program in the ability to anticipate, call attention to, and even correct defects in processing, as well as more complex manufacturing operations.

Computers are now being used in legal research, but the legal profession will soon find more uses for them. Language translation is a reality, though really in its infancy. Practical and low-cost visual display systems will be available shortly which will allow an executive to make an inquiry and then immediately view the requested data on his private screen. Voice communication from the computer is already a practical request, and we may even choose the gender of the vocal response.

The Promise and the Challenge

Certain it is that still more wonderful inventions and innovations will be made available to management. It will therefore be wise to admit the impossibility of predicting the extent to which computers of the future will affect the lives of coming generations. But with every joy, according to the law of balance, there must be a compensating responsibility. Management's responsibilities of the future will be fearsome things, for with the advent of more glamorous equipment comes the threat of even greater waste.

One definition of the word "ignorant" is "lacking knowledge or information as to a particular subject or fact." So there is nothing derogatory about the admission that we are ignorant of many things. Computers have been one of the subjects on which management lacks knowledge. This ignorance we can afford no longer. As computers get bigger and more complex, the possibilities of waste increase alarmingly; and such waste is not congruent with our system of things. Capitalism and democracy go hand in hand, and neither can exist without the other. Sadly enough, capitalism cannot sustain itself in an environment of waste without making democracy suffer. We will find more and more, as time progresses, that computers will become either a deterrent or a boon in maintaining this delicate balance.

Reference to the waste of the past is not an indictment of the inventive genius of the computer designers and manufacturers. The doctor who discovers a new miracle drug cannot be condemned because his discovery is misused through ignorance. Doctors have learned to use the magic of discovery; so must management learn to utilize the new tools at its disposal.

One thing is clear: Modularity in future computers is as certain as the law of supply and demand. Special-purpose computers will be designed to stand alone or constitute part of a bigger system so that operation may be separate for the small user. Flexibility will be stressed in machine systems but somewhat de-emphasized in the component parts. This will, strangely enough, provide more overall flexibility and lower cost because greater volume production will be possible.

Throughout all this, the intelligent and courageous manager will ask questions of the technician, and together knowledge will be shared. And increased knowledge will in turn lead to more intelligent use of the machines to produce a satisfactory return on investment. The department store manager may not care about a system which can tell him in three seconds that counter 5 is out of size 9 cotton socks, but the sales executive of an airline will want to know immediately when five seats are available on a flight from Chicago to New York. Common sense? Yes, and common sense is a commodity which has been all too uncommon in the use of computers.

Needed: Manager with a Broad Viewpoint

Not too long ago, an article on data processing management which appeared in a widely read journal predicted that the manager with the broad viewpoint would be replaced by the technical type. Perhaps—but by a technically oriented manager with a broad viewpoint. After all, engineers have become very successful businessmen; accountants, good corporation presidents. Leaders are leaders wherever they come from and wherever they are found.

Somewhere up the line there must still be that broad-gauge man. He will be with us a long time, for he is the driving force behind real accomplishment in all things, including data processing. He will always be the man who makes the big decisions, informed or otherwise, which will shape the future of computer equipment as a management tool. He will determine responsibility and accountability —the charge and discharge of managership. He will view data processing equipment as a means to an end, but not as an end in itself. And he will know that policy is important. Only when it is well established can systems be intelligently and effectively designed.

This is the executive to whom this book is directed—the man who has little time to concern himself with detail but who must face bravely, and possibly with a feeling of ineptness, the responsibility for data processing.

There is little of management science which can be imparted here to a man of experience. It is our intent, rather, to offer some reassurance that the management of data processing is little different from management in other areas. The machines may be frightening, yes; so are jet airliners. But, though we have no detailed knowledge of the aircraft, we step on board with confidence in the ability of the pilot. We know what the plane will do under the pilot's expert guidance—and he knows where we wish to go. Just so, the data processing technician is our pilot. Though we have no detailed knowledge of computers, he will take us where we wish to go—if we tell him our destination.

As in many other endeavors, there is a critical need for good technicians, and the effective manager will have the foresight to flavor the job with real interest supported by informed leadership—and with deserved monetary rewards. He will provide opportunities for advancement out of data processing when a man reaches the top; in fact, he will actively encourage the goal of broader knowledge in company problems to improve the likelihood of advancement—and more intelligent equipment utilization.

If we help our data processing people to understand our other operational problems, we will have less trouble with the "big spenders," those who would order equipment only because it is more glamorous.

The wise executive will recognize that machines which today provide solutions in the world of business and science in nanoseconds (billionths of a second) have failed to unravel the knotty problems of management by speed alone. He will also perceive, because he has wisdom and foresight, that machines of the future operating in picoseconds (trillionths of a second) will do little more to solve management problems purely because of their lightning speed. Nor will the coming of laser light circuitry offer any help for a management that fails to keep its sights set on its primary responsibility—to provide learned leadership in a very important endeavor.

PART TWO:

Technical Session

*Part Two, although we call it "Technical Session,"
actually is intended to cover only the bare essentials
of computers: their make-up, the mathematics involved, the elementary logic of planning and preparing to program the job. It will also introduce the
reader to methods of checks and balances inside and
outside the machine. One should not expect to emerge
from these pages as an accomplished programer or
machine technician. It is our hope that Part Two
will, however, help to increase the confidence of the
executive who has pressed his nose against the computer room window but has been afraid to enter,
much less ask questions.*

18. What Is a Computer System?

A BUSINESS SYSTEM INSTALLED ON A COMPUTER APPEARS TO BE complex, but the rudiments are easily understood when described as they apply to a familiar job. We shall start by examining the methods used in the manual preparation of a payroll.

The clerk who computes the payroll manually has available the following "master" information:

EXHIBIT 1

For week ending: *12/11*

Employee Name	Clock No.	Hours Worked	Hourly Rate	Gross Pay	Tax Rate	WH Tax Deduction	Bond Deduction	Total Deduction	Net Pay
Leonard Foss	*4176*		*1.75*		*.18*		*3.00*		
Albert Gross	*4192*		*2.20*		*.18*		*5.00*		
John Mellon	*4198*		*2.15*		*.18*		—		
Joe Milner	*4201*		*1.95*		*.18*		*4.50*		
Jack Smith	*4202*		*1.95*		*.18*		*2.00*		
Mike Stern	*4212*		*2.00*		*.22*		*1.00*		

If we were to write down the instructions our clerk follows in processing the payroll, they would appear in this sequence:

1. From weekly time card record the hours worked in the column "Hours Worked."
2. Multiply hours worked by hourly rate to get gross pay.
3. Record gross pay in column "Gross Pay."
4. Multiply gross pay by tax rate to get withholding tax deduction.
5. Record WH tax deduction in column "WH Tax Deduction."
6. Add WH tax deduction to bond deduction to get total deduction.

139

7. Record total deduction in column "Total Deduction."

8. Subtract total deduction from gross pay to get net pay.

9. Record net pay in column "Net Pay."

In actual practice, the clerk will likely perform instruction 1 for all employees before advancing to instruction 2. So as to compare this job later to a computer routine, we shall assume that he performs all nine instructions on one employee before proceeding to the next.

By putting column numbers on the payroll form, we can write our nine instructions in condensed form:

EXHIBIT 2

← Column Numbers →									
1	2	3	4	5	6	7	8	9	10
Employee Name	Clock No.	Hours Worked	Hourly Rate	Gross Pay	Tax Rate	WH Tax Deduction	Bond Deduction	Total Deduction	Net Pay
Leonard Foss	4176		1.75		.18		3.00		
Albert Gross	4192		2.20		.18		5.00		
John Mellon	4198		2.15		.18		—		
Joe Milner	4201		1.95		.18		4.50		
Jack Smith	4202		1.95		.18		2.00		
Mike Stern	4212		2.00		.22		1.00		

Now the instructions can be written in this way:

1. From weekly time card (input) copy the hours worked in column 3.
2. Multiply the number in column 3 by the number in column 4.
3. Record answer in column 5.
4. Multiply the number in column 5 by the rate in column 6.
5. Record answer in column 7.
6. Add the number in column 7 to the number in column 8.
7. Record answer in column 9.
8. Subtract number in column 9 from number in column 5.
9. Record answer in column 10.

These instructions can be further condensed if we take the liberty of omitting the words "the number in." However, we must keep in mind that the column numbers we now show represent a label or address somewhat similar to the numbered mail boxes in a post office and that we are dealing with the contents of the address specified.

When we write the number "4," we mean "the contents of column 4." Hence our instructions become:

1. From weekly time card record hours worked in 3.
2. Multiply 3 by 4.
3. Record answer in 5.
4. Multiply 5 by 6.
5. Record answer in 7.
6. Add 7 to 8.
7. Record answer in 9.
8. Subtract 9 from 5.
9. Record answer in 10.

Since everyone is familiar with arithmetic symbols, we could write instructions 2 through 9 in a symbolic manner. Starting with instruction 2:

2. $3 \times 4 = 5$.
3. $5 \times 6 = 7$.
4. $7 + 8 = 9$.
5. $5 - 9 = 10$.

These abbreviated instructions can be made a part of the form itself.

The form shown initially (Exhibit 1) contained information which is generally referred to as *the data to be processed*. This information, condensed (Exhibit 2), consists of the basic (or master) data. To it are added the instructions on how these data are to be processed (Exhibit 3). These instructions make up the *program*.

EXHIBIT 3

For week ending: *12/11*

1	2	3	4	5	6	7	8	9	10
			3 x 4		5 x 6			7 + 8	5 − 9
Employee Name	Clock No.	Hours Worked	Hourly Rate	Gross Pay	Tax Rate	WH Tax Deduction	Bond Deduction	Total Deduction	Net Pay
Leonard Foss	4176		1.75		.18		3.00		
Albert Gross	4192		2.20		.18		5.00		
John Mellon	4198		2.15		.18				
Joe Milner	4201		1.95		.18		4.50		
Jack Smith	4202		1.95		.18		2.00		
Mike Stern	4212		2.00		.22		1.00		

We have stipulated that the clerk is to go through all nine operations on each employee before advancing to the next. This means that he can perform the job on a form just large enough to hold the data pertaining to one employee.

We shall ignore the shaded portion of the form shown in Exhibit 4. Instead of numbering each column, we have now numbered each box—boxes 01 through 10 being comparable to the previously used columns on employee information (the data to be processed), while boxes 11 through 20 are comparable to the top row of the form shown in Exhibit 3. Boxes 15, 17, 19, and 20 contain the four instructions developed to this point. Other boxes still blank will be used to record additional instructions and data as we progress through the problem.

EXHIBIT 4

For week ending: *12/11*

11	12	13	14	3x4 15	16	5x6 17	18	7+8 19	5-9 20
1	2	3	4	5	6	7	8	9	10
Employee Name	Clock No.	Hours Worked	Hourly Rate	Gross Pay	Tax Rate	WH Tax Deduction	Bond Deduction	Total Deduction	Net Pay
Leonard Foss 01	4176 02	03	1.75 04	05	.18 06	07	3.00 08	09	10
Albert Gross	4192		2.20		.18		5.00		
John Mellon	4198		2.15		.18		—		
Joe Milner	4201		1.95		.18		4.50		
Jack Smith	4202		1.95		.18		2.00		
Mike Stern	4212		2.00		.22		1.00		

Boxes 01 through 20 are now sufficient to process one employee; therefore, we can replace our original form with the one shown in Exhibit 5.

EXHIBIT 5

For week ending: *12/11*

11	12	13	14	15 03x04=05	16	17 05x06=07	18	19 07+08=09	20 05-09=10
01 Leonard Foss	02 4176	03	04 1.75	05	06 .18	07	08 3.00	09	10

Note that where the column widths on the original form were variable, we have now made them uniform. When the data were brought to the form and recorded, assignments were made so that employee name (Leonard Foss) went to box 01; clock number went to box (or address) 02; hourly rate went to address 04; and so forth. The *program* (stored in addresses 15, 17, 19, and 20) will describe how the data in addresses 01 through 10 will be processed. After completion of the processing for Leonard Foss (and the subsequent writing of the check), the data in *locations* 01 through 10 will be replaced with the data for the next employee, Albert Gross. The *stored* program, however, will remain in locations 15, 17, 19, and 20 so that it may be used to process variable data on the second employee (Albert Gross) and for the remaining names in turn.

Before we compute the net pay for Leonard Foss it will be necessary to enter the variable data (hours worked) into location 03. The instruction could be entered into any one of the unused addresses 11 through 20, but for this example let us place it in 13. Using the worksheet-type form in Exhibit 6, the clerk (or programer) will write the instruction "Enter hours in 03" in location 13.

EXHIBIT 6

For week ending: *12/11*

11	12	13	14	15	16	17	18	19	20
		Enter hours in 03		03x04=05		05x06=07		07+08=09	05-09=10
01	02	03	04	05	06	07	08	09	10
Leonard Foss	4176	40.0	1.75	70.00	.18	12.60	3.00	15.60	54.40

To start processing, we begin with the instruction in 13. After its *execution,* we have 40.0 recorded in 03, assuming this employee worked 40.0 hours during the week. Then we go to instruction 15, whose execution will result in the recording of 70.00 in 05. Continuing on to the instructions in 17, 19, and 20 in that order, we develop the results 12.60, 15.60, and 54.40 in locations 07, 09, and 10.

At this point net pay has been computed on the worksheet. The need satisfied by this entire operation was to create a check for the employee; so the data in locations 01 through 10 must then be transferred to the check blank. The instruction could be placed in lo-

cation 21 if available on the worksheet; but, since there are only 20
locations, and since 11 is as yet unused, we can place it there. We
shall direct execution of instruction 11 after instruction 20. The
instruction "Record 01 through 10 on check blank" is written in
location 11; and, when the instruction is carried out, a check will be
created for Leonard Foss. (See Exhibit 7, which also shows the instruction, in location 12, to bring in the basic data for the next employee, Albert Gross.)

EXHIBIT 7

For week ending : *12/11*

11 Record 01 through 10 on check blank	12 Enter next basic data in 01-02- 04-06-08	13 Enter hours in 03	14	15 03×04=05	16	17 05×06=07	18	19 07+08=09	20 05-09=10
01 * *Albert Gross*	02 * *4192*	03 *40.0*	04 * *2.20*	05 *70.00*	06 * *.18*	07 *12.60*	08 * *5.00*	09 *15.60*	10 *54.40*

* Basic information on second employee. See text.

To read the new data into locations 01, 02, 04, 06, and 08 requires
that the old data in these locations be erased. In a computer the new
data read into a location automatically erase any data previously
stored there. (Note that 03, 05, 07, 09, and 10 in Exhibit 7 still contain the data pertaining to the previous employee, Leonard Foss.)
Then, after the instruction in 12 is executed, the instructions in 13,
15, 17, 19, and 20 are executed as shown in Exhibit 8, erasing the old
computations as shown.

In the process of creating a check for each employee, the clerk will
have performed the job as follows:

1. *Input:* Recording of basic data in 01, 02, 04, 06, 08; recording
   of hours worked in 03.
2. *Arithmetic:* Instructions in 15, 17, 19, and 20 involving
   multiply, add, and subtract functions—possibly requiring the
   use of an adding machine or a desk calculator.
3. *Output:* The instruction in 11; transfer of the data from the
   worksheet to a check blank.

In performing these three functions, the clerk used the worksheet to *record* and *store* the data being processed. This worksheet served as a *storage media*.

EXHIBIT 8

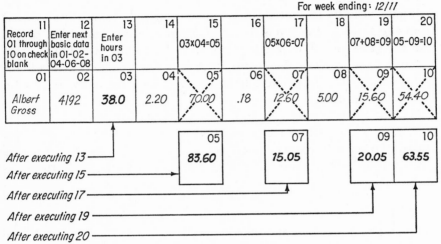

For week ending: *12/11*

11 Record 01 through 10 on check blank	12 Enter next basic data in 01-02-04-06-08	13 Enter hours in 03	14	15 03x04=05	16	17 05x06=07	18	19 07+08=09	20 05-09=10
01 Albert Gross	02 4192	03 **38.0**	04 2.20	05 70.00	06 .18	07 12.60	08 5.00	09 15.60	10 54.40

	05 **83.60**	07 **15.05**	09 **20.05**	10 **63.55**

After executing 13

After executing 15

After executing 17

After executing 19

After executing 20

Instruction in 11 will record 01 through 10 data on the second employee on a check blank.

Instruction in 12 will begin a new cycle.

Computer make-up includes five basic elements, four of which are *input, arithmetic, output,* and *storage*. To link these four elements, the control unit of the computer provides for the interpretation and execution of each instruction, for communication and transfer of information to and from the other elements, and for the activation of input and output devices at the proper time. The clerk could be called the control unit.

From Exhibit 5 on, you will recall, the widths of the columns were made uniform. Thus each column on the form will accept the same number of letters or digits; for example, each block or address as shown might be made large enough to contain a maximum of 12 characters (letters or digits), as is the case in location 01.

In the case of location 06, where only two digits are required (tax rate), we will still have the 12-character capacity even though only two are used. The remaining ten positions in this location may be considered as containing zeros. The length, or capacity, of each address in a computer is referred to as *word length*. Each word in a computer has an *address,* which is comparable to the addresses (box numbers) shown in our examples. In a word machine, all words are of equal size; however, the word size may vary from computer to computer.

In processing the first employee (clock number 4176), the clerk will have visually extracted the hourly rate ($1.75) and hours worked from the form and entered the amounts into a desk machine to obtain the gross pay. The fact that the clerk "read out" the hourly rate did not erase it from the form; likewise, when a word is read out from storage in a computer, it is not erased or removed. It can be read over and over.

When the clerk was ready to record gross pay into 05, this location had some previously written information in it which had to be erased. To record or store data in a computer word, any information already there will be automatically erased and replaced by the new entry.

The *stored program* on the form in Exhibit 5 is very generalized. In a computer the program would be located in pre-assigned locations and would be composed primarily of "instruction" words. In our example, location 15 would contain an instruction word and 04 a data word. Any location or address in computer storage can be occupied by either an instruction or a data word. An instruction word will usually be made up of an *operation code* or *command,* a *data address,* and a *next instruction address.* An operation code (or command) is usually a two-, three-, or four-digit code which represents a given operation in the computer; for example, "70" might mean "Read a card"; "15," "Add to accumulator"; and so on. The data address of an instruction word refers to the address where the data are contained. For example, "15 0019" might mean "Add to accumulator the contents of location 0019." The next instruction address will be the address of the next instruction to be carried out. In some computers this address is a part of the instruction word; in others it is not.

19. The Components
Of the Computer

In the previous chapter we discussed a simple payroll problem and related it to the five basic elements of a computer: input, storage, control, arithmetic, and output.

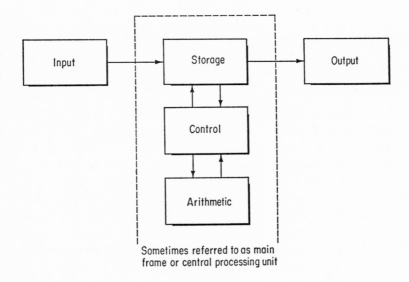

Sometimes referred to as main
frame or central processing unit

Input

The term "input" suggests two physical acts: first, the preparation of the medium on which the data are recorded (for entry into the computer) and, second, the use of a mechanical device to read these data and transmit them to the computer. The most common

147

input media are punched cards, paper tape, magnetic tape, character recognition, and keyboard (or console).

Punched cards. The two common types of punched cards are the 80-column and the 90-column. The 80-column card can have recorded on it, in the form of punched holes, up to 80 characters. A character is a number, a letter, or a special character such as −, @, or /. Exhibit 1 shows an 80-column card and the codes associated with each number and letter. The Hollerith system is used.

EXHIBIT 1
PUNCHED CARD (HOLLERITH CODE)

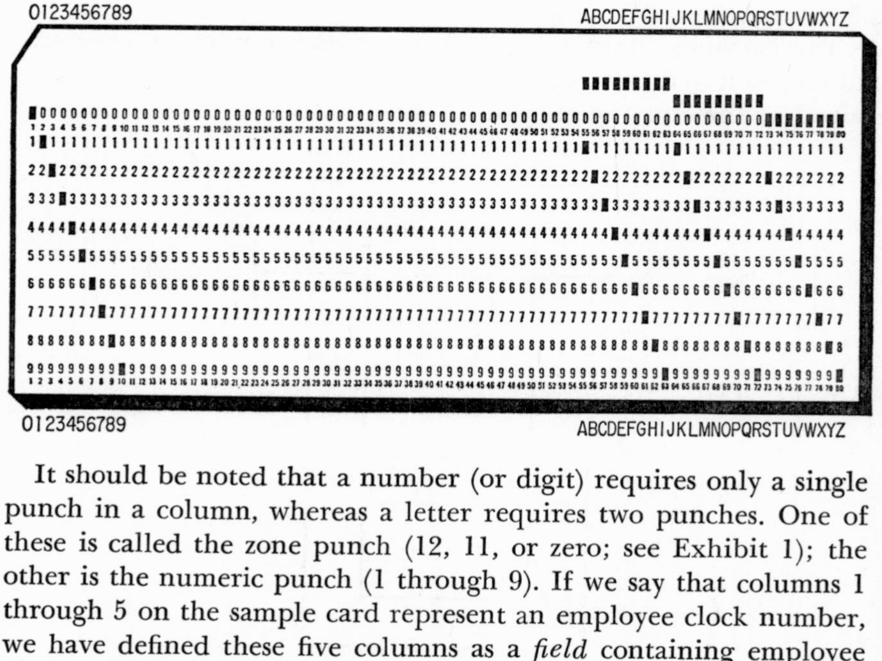

It should be noted that a number (or digit) requires only a single punch in a column, whereas a letter requires two punches. One of these is called the zone punch (12, 11, or zero; see Exhibit 1); the other is the numeric punch (1 through 9). If we say that columns 1 through 5 on the sample card represent an employee clock number, we have defined these five columns as a *field* containing employee number 01234.

A *card reader* is used to read and transmit the data from the card to computer storage. Generally, the reader makes use of wire brushes or photo-electric cells to sense the holes in the card, and reading is done in a "parallel" fashion; that is, a separate circuit is available for each column and all 80 columns are read simultaneously. If only one circuit was available and all the columns had to be read through it in turn (column 1 first, column 2 second, column 3 next, and so on), then we would be using *series-* or *serial-*type reading.

Paper tape. Punched paper tape is a strip of paper, maintained in folded stacks or on round reels, in which a pattern of holes is punched. This tape can be of various widths, usually from 11/16 to approximately 1 inch. There is no universal code for paper tape. Two different systems are commonly used: the five-channel teletype (Baudot) code and the more popular (computerwise) eight-channel code.

EXHIBIT 2
FIVE-CHANNEL PAPER TAPE

Teletype Code Tape	Figures Shift Characters	Letters Shift Characters
	φ	P
	1	Q
	2	W
	3	E
	4	R
	5	T
	6	Y
	7	U
	8	I
	9	O
	+	Z
	−	A
	.	M
	Tab/CR	Car. Ret
	/	X
	)	L
	:	C
	,	N
	!	F
	s	S
	H	H
	$	D
	&	G
	(	K
	Fig. Shift	Fig. Shift
	;	V
	?	B
	Ltr. Shift	Ltr. Shift
	Line Feed	Line Feed
	Space	Space
	Blank	Blank
	,	ɪ

Exhibit 2 shows the coding for the five-channel teletype code. Since five channels can represent only 32 different combinations ($2^5 = 32$) and there are 36 characters (26 letters plus 10 digits) to be represented, use is made of the *figures shift* to record the digits and special characters shown in the "Figures Shift" column. Letters are recorded when operating the letters shift mode. The result is similar to that obtained by using the shift key on a typewriter.

The coding for the eight-channel tape is illustrated in Exhibit 3.

EXHIBIT 3

EIGHT-CHANNEL PAPER TAPE

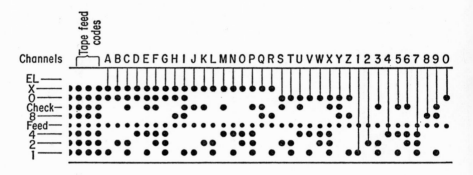

Six channels (1,2,4,8,0,X) are used to record any number, letter, or special character. The channel marked "Check" is intended to satisfy a validity check and will contain a punch whenever the basic code (1,2,4,8,0,X) consists of an even number of holes. The check hole is then added to make an odd number of holes so that every column can be checked when reading for the presence of an odd count. The "EL" channel is automatically punched to mark the end of a line or record on the tape. The lower four channels of the tape, excluding the sprocket or feed holes, are used to record numerical characters. For example, a hole in channel 2 represents a numerical "2." A combination of a "1" and a "2" punch represents a numerical "3." The X and 0 channels are used in combination with the numerical channels in recording alphabetic and special characters like the zone punches in the punched card previously discussed. Paper tape can be read directly into a computer by a *paper tape reader* or "converted" to magnetic tape for introduction to the computer.

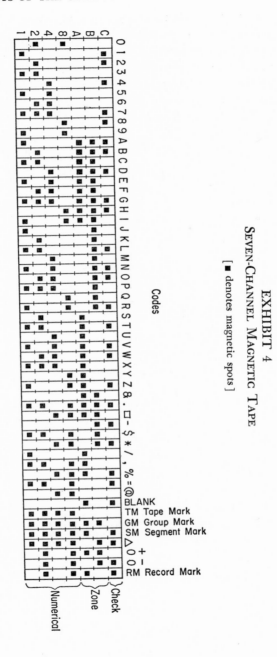

EXHIBIT 4
SEVEN-CHANNEL MAGNETIC TAPE

[■ denotes magnetic spots]

Magnetic tape. There is a decided lack of uniformity in magnetic tape used with the computer. There are plastic and metallic types, widths can vary from half an inch up to three inches, and the representation of characters can differ widely.

Data are represented on magnetic tape by combinations of magnetic spots, so small that more than 1,500 spots may be recorded on a thin pencil line one inch long. Most commonly used is the seven-channel tape (four numeric, two zone, and one check). Exhibit 4 illustrates a seven-channel tape showing the bit (magnetic spot) combinations used for the various characters.

Magnetic tape is written or read into storage by a magnetic tape unit or drive at a rate, on most modern equipment, varying from 15,000 up to 340,000 characters per second. (See Exhibit 4.)

Character recognition devices. The advantage of character recognition is that neither keypunching nor any other manual operation is necessary to produce machine language.

There are two types of character recognition devices, magnetic and optical. A good example of magnetic character usage is probably to be found on your personal checks, since most modern banks now make use of this type of input. Optical methodology is illustrated by your oil company credit card, where raised numbers are used to produce the charge information on sales slips which will later be read optically.

This method of input will become more popular as time goes on because processing requires a minimum of human intervention and clerical cost between the source of the data and the computer.

Keyboard or console. Information can be entered manually into all general-purpose computers through the use of a keyboard (typewriter or special) or a console where dial-type switches are used to set up the desired information. Since this type of input is slow, it is used sparingly—primarily for inserting changes or new constants (such as a date) into a program in the memory.

Storage

Storage, or *memory,* is the part of a computer in which information (digits or letters) is stored. Three common types of storage are (1) magnetic core, (2) magnetic drum, (3) magnetic disc. A fourth and new type, in limited use at present, is thin film.

Magnetic core. Core is made up of small ferromagnetic rings, perhaps .080 inch in diameter and .025 inch thick. These rings have properties which allow energizing in either of two directions; that is, the core can be positively charged or negatively charged. If the current direction for minus is as shown in Exhibit 5A, then the core through

EXHIBIT 5

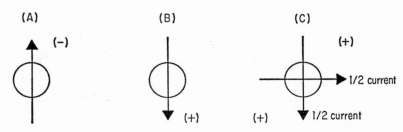

(A) (B) (C)

which this current passes is negatively charged. If the current were reversed, the core could be said to be positively charged (Exhibit 5B)—as it could be, also, if we were to reduce the current by half and give it the two directions shown in Exhibit 5C. Thus we have the ability to charge selectively only certain cores in the *core plane*.

Suppose, as in Exhibit 6, there are nine cores arranged as shown and current is allowed to flow along the boldface lines. Then the core at the intersection of these two wires would be the only core to be positively charged.

EXHIBIT 6

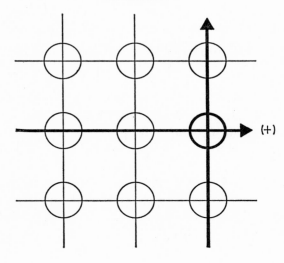

EXHIBIT 7

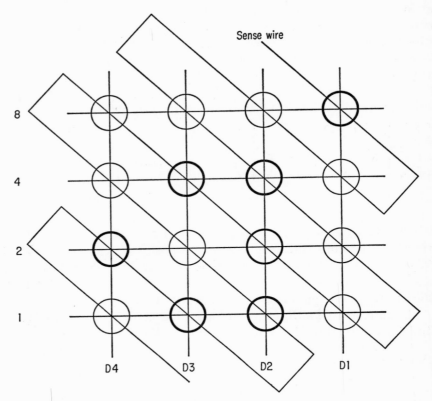

But consider now a four-by-four matrix as in Exhibit 7. Assume that the four horizontal lines are given values 1, 2, 4, and 8 as shown and that the vertical lines represent the four digits of an amount; for example, D1 represents the units position, D2 the tens position, and so forth. To store, or record, the number "8" in the units position (D1), we would allow current to flow along horizontal line 8 and vertical line D1. Core 8 on line D1 would then be positively charged. After setting up the units position, we would proceed to the tens position and allow current to flow in line D2 and the horizontal lines required to represent the tens digit in our four-digit amount. If this figure were a "7," then current would be passed in lines 1, 2, and 4—which three add up to, and represent, a "7." The three cores at the intersection of the current-passing wires would be charged. The process would continue on to line D3 and then to line D4. In the example shown, the amount 2578 is stored in memory.

Read-out is accomplished by the addition of a third wire, called the *sense wire,* which is threaded diagonally through the cores. Once a core has been charged, it will retain this charge without current until some later read-in takes place. Writing (or recording) and reading speeds are extremely fast.

Magnetic drum. Information may also be stored in magnetic spots on the surface of a rotating drum. Reading and writing of these magnetic spots are then accomplished by devices, known as *read-write heads,* which are mounted on bars around the drum. Any magnetized spot recorded on the drum will remain there permanently, or until it is erased by recording in the same location, and the machine may be turned off completely without losing it from the drum's surface.

The time required to record or read information by means of drum storage is longer than for core storage since *wait time* (usually figured at half the time of a revolution) is necessary for the given address to reach and pass under the read-write heads.

Magnetic disc. Disc storage is somewhat similar to a phonograph record rotating on a vertical spindle. The information is read (or written) by a read-write head much like the arm on a record player; it is recorded on the disc in the form of magnetized spots on tracks. The disc, or discs, are permanently mounted on most equipment and cannot be removed or replaced as on a home record player, although smaller units which are now available feature removable discs. Addresses are made available by dividing the disc into tracks and sectors.

Thin film. At this date thin film is not widely used for computer memory. In laymen's terms it may be compared to a printed circuit on a very thin material arranged in much the same way as core. Its advantages, other than speed measured in nanoseconds, include the ability to store a tremendous amount of data in a very small stack of thin film sheets.

Other methods of storage will be developed, but certain fundamentals will not change. Storage, to be useful, must be divided into addressable increments in much the same manner as mail-sorting pigeonholes. These compartments are referred to as *words,* each word having its own *address.* As previously mentioned, the size of a word may vary from computer to computer. In some, it is one character and, as a result, each character is addressable. These are sometimes referred to as *character* machines as opposed to *word* machines.

In a machine utilizing a fixed word length, the question arises as to how fields (such as clock number) and the computer word are to be related when they most likely will be of different lengths. As a matter of fact, a six-digit clock number can be recorded in a ten-digit word, leaving zeros to occupy the remaining four positions. It is also possible to allocate the six low-order (or high-order) digits of the word to store the clock number and use the remaining four digits to store a four-digit unit number. Thus two fields have been placed in one word. When each of these fields is to be operated on arithmetically, the word will be *unpacked* by the program to separate them. Conversely, two or more fields are combined in one word by *packing*. But where a field (such as part number) is longer than the computer word, an additional word or words will be needed to store it.

Control

The control element of a computer directs it during the complete process of problem solution. It determines the sequence of operations, interprets them, and activates the input and output devices. To perform these functions an instruction word must be read from the stored program and held in the control element while the word is being interpreted and the instruction carried out. The device used by the control element to hold or contain this instruction word is usually referred to as a *register*.

Generally there are several registers, and the name associated with each one derives from the function it performs. For example, a register which stores the entire instruction word may be called a *program* register; and, if the operation code is extracted and placed in another register for interpretation and setup, it may be referred to as an *operation* register. In the same way a register which stores an address and provides for setting up the circuits to communicate with this address may be referred to as an *address* register. All these are registers containing control or instruction information; in the section dealing with the arithmetic element of the computer we shall see that registers there contain operands for some arithmetic process.

When reading information from card or paper tape readers into computer storage, there is generally a great difference in the operating speeds of the reader and the ability of the computer to accept and store. A card reader operating at 400 cards per minute will require 150 milliseconds to read each card, while the computer could accept and store this same information much faster. If we provide some intermediate means of storage—that is, between the reader and the computer storage—sufficient to hold one card's information, and if we allow this to fill up during the 150 milliseconds' read time before we call it into computer storage, then we need, for example, only 10 microseconds of computer time to achieve read-in. This is referred to as *buffered* input, and the intermediate storage used is called a *buffer*. Both output and input may be buffered.

Arithmetic

The arithmetic element is the computing portion of the system. The operations of addition, subtraction, multiplication, and division are performed by this element, as well as comparisons which give the computer its ability to perform logical operations. Registers are required for the storage of a data word (or operand) while it is being processed according to the command associated with it. A very common term used in referring to this type of register is *accumulator;* through it the actual addition or subtraction of two numbers is accomplished. Generally two or more accumulators are employed, and these are addressable in the same manner as a word in storage.

Output

Computer output, like input, involves two things: (1) the medium on which the output is recorded and (2) the machine or device required to accept data from memory and create the output record. The types of output to be considered here are punched cards, punched paper tape, magnetic tape, printed report, and console.

Punched cards. Cards containing the output data in the form of punched holes, coded as described under "input," are created by a *card punch.* Card punches operate generally in the range of 100 to 250 cards per minute.

Punched paper tape. Paper tape, also coded as described under "input," is created by a *paper tape punch.* Operating speeds generally range from 20 to 240 characters per second.

Magnetic tape. The section on magnetic tape under "input" applies here as well.

Printed report. Translation of data from computer memory to a printed sheet which we can read is performed by a *printer*. Generally, printers turn out a line at a time (up to 132 characters) at a rate up to 1,200 lines per minute (more by some processes).

Quite often, typewriters are used (sometimes they are referred to as *character-at-a-time printers*) to print out limited data.

Console. Small lights on the console are frequently used to display the contents of some part of the stored information. These lights may be direct-reading; that is, a "3," for example, is actually displayed. More commonly, however, certain combinations of lights will indicate the number; for instance, if the light farthest to the right in a group of four is on, the number represented could be a "1," while if the one on the extreme left is the only light showing, the number could be an "8."

The use of the console for output is usually limited to operator convenience in determining the reasons for computer stoppage, programer convenience in debugging a new program, or maintenance.

20. Number Systems and How They Work

$\mathbf{D}$IGITAL COMPUTERS' USE BINARY CIRCUITS; THEREFORE, THE MATH-
ematics of the computer is binary in nature. The binary system
is used because the "yes or no" logic is compatible with "on or off"
electrical characteristics. A relay maintains its contacts either closed
or open; magnetic materials are utilized by putting them in a negative or positive state; a vacuum tube is conveniently maintained as
either fully conducting or nonconducting; and the transmission of
information along a wire may be accomplished by transmitting or
eliminating an electrical pulse at a certain time.

Simply defined, the word "binary" means "consisting of two things
or parts." Applying this to our computer components (relays, tubes,
and the like) where only two conditions can be represented (contacts
closed or open, tubes conducting or nonconducting), we see how
convenient it is to use a system of numbers consisting of only two
digits rather than the ten digits in our decimal system.

Let us consider the following quantity of x's:

xxxxxxxxxxxxxxxxxxxxxxxxxxxxxxx

To convey in understandable language how many x's are represented here (actually there are 31), suppose we lump them together
and refer to the result as a *basket*. If we agree that each basket shall
contain, say, ten x's, then we find that we can describe our total as
"three baskets and one left over"; or, as we could have said at the
outset, "31." This is the number system we are all familiar with:
the decimal system calling for groups of ten.

On the other hand, suppose we define the size of the basket so

159

that it will contain only eight x's. We can still fill up only three baskets, but this time we have seven x's left over. In this system, then, we have a quantity of "37," but we must be sure to indicate that it is a number "to the base 8"; that is, we counted in groups of eight. This number system is referred to as the *octal* system. In the case of the decimal system we need make no special notation because of its universal usage, but this same quantity expressed octally must be written "$37_{(8)}$."

If the basket contained six x's, we would have five baskets and one left over. Expressed numerically this would be "$51_{(6)}$." But suppose we let each basket contain four x's. Our first reaction might be to say we have seven baskets and three left over; however, this would not be valid because there are no numbers higher than "3" in our language. We need to go back and look at our decimal system again.

In the decimal system we have ten digits—0 through 9. By means of these we can express a quantity of as many as nine baskets (99), but if we have more baskets than this we introduce a new unit of measure—hundreds—and show it by moving one place to the left.

Likewise, if we have a number system based on only four digits—actually 0 through 3—we cannot express the quantity of baskets in excess of three by using a digit that is not valid to this system. As in the decimal system, we need to introduce new units of measure to the left as each one to the right spills over. Although it is similar to the hundreds position in the decimal system, we shall, for our purpose here, introduce a new unit which we call *tub*. So, returning to our original quantity (31), we find we have two tubs, three baskets, and three left over. Therefore, this quantity could be expressed as "$233_{(4)}$"; that is, $(2 \times 8) + (3 \times 4) + (3 \times 1) = 31$.

Consider now, however, that our basket will contain just two x's. Since we have only two digits—0 and 1—we need to develop new units of measure in addition to the tub. Listed below are the units to be used in our discussion; also shown are the comparable names used in our decimal system.

> Let 1 basket = xx
>   2 baskets = 1 tub
>   2 tubs   = 1 barrel
>   2 barrels = 1 tank.

The original quantity of x's (31) can now be described as "one tank,

one barrel, one tub, one basket, and one left over," or "$11111_{(2)}$."
This is the binary number system.

Binary-System Computations

Although binary numbers have more terms than their decimal
counterparts, machine computation in the binary mode is quite
simple. For addition it is only necessary to remember the following
rules:

Zero plus zero equals zero.

Zero plus one equals one.

One plus one equals zero, with a carry of one to the next position
on the left.

To see how the rules work, consider the addition of 15 plus 7 with
these numbers expressed in binary notation:

	Sixteens	Eights	Fours	Twos	Ones
(carries)	(1)	(1)	(1)	(1)	
	0	1	1	1	1 = 15
+0	0	1	1	1 = 7
	1	0	1	1	0 = 22

In the "Ones" column we have 1 plus 1 for a sum of 0 and a 1
carried to the "Twos" column. In the "Twos" column we have 1 plus
1 for a sum of 0, but we must also add the carry from the "Ones"
column, making a final sum of 1 with a carry to the "Fours" column.
The same procedure occurs in the "Fours" column. In the "Eights"
column we have 1 plus 0, giving a sum of 1, but adding in the carry
from the "Fours" column makes the final sum 0 with a carry to the
"Sixteens" column. In this column we have 0 plus 0, giving a sum
of 0, and to this we add the carry from the "Eights" column,
making a final sum of 1. The resulting sum of the addition contains
"1's" in the "Sixteens," "Fours," and "Twos" columns, which is the
binary representation of 22, the correct sum of 15 plus 7 (16 plus
4 plus 2 equals 22).

The rules for subtraction of binary digits are equally simple:

Zero minus zero equals zero.

One minus one equals zero.

One minus zero equals one.

Zero minus one equals one, with one borrowed from the left.

Using the same numbers as for addition, the process is as follows:

	Sixteens	Eights	Fours	Twos	Ones
(borrows)	0	0	0	0	
	0	1	1	1	1 = 15
	−0	0	1	1	1 = 7
	0	1	0	0	0 = 8

In the "Ones" column we have 1 minus 1, leaving 0 with no borrows. The same procedure occurs in the "Twos" and "Fours" columns. In the "Eights" column we have 1 minus 0, leaving a balance of 1. In the "Sixteens" column we have 0 minus 0, leaving 0. With the subtraction finished we have 1's in the "Eights" column only; thus our answer is 8.

For multiplication only three rules need to be remembered:

Zero times zero equals zero.

Zero times one equals zero; no carries are considered.

One times one equals one.

The binary multiplication table is such that all that is necessary when multiplying one number (multiplicand) by another (multiplier) is to examine the multiplier digits one at a time and, each time a "1" is found, add the multiplicand into the result and, each time a "0" is found, add nothing. Of course the multiplicand must be shifted for each multiplier digit, but this is no different from the shifting done in the decimal system. As an example, take the problem of multiplying 26 by 19:

Decimal System	Binary System
$26 = 16 + 8 + 0 + 2 + 0 =$	11010
$\times 19 = 16 + 0 + 0 + 2 + 1 =$	10011
	11010
	11010
	00000
	00000
	11010
	111101110

Interpreting the binary result by using our system of 1's, 2's, 4's, and so on, we find that we have $256 + 128 + 64 + 32 + 0 + 8 + 4 + 2 + 0$. This equals 494, thus proving the problem.

Binary division is accomplished by applying similar concepts. Generally speaking, from our description of addition, subtraction, and multiplication it may be seen that whatever operation the computer performs will necessarily be done by means of repetitive addition.

The computer operates internally by means of the binary system. However, it is able to convert from one system to another by using a stored interpretive program. This means that input-output data may be expressed in decimal or other systems when the operator finds it more convenient to do so.

The Octal System and the Computer

It has already been pointed out that binary numbers require more than three times as many positions as decimal numbers to express the same quantity. This is not a problem to the computer. In talking and writing, however, binary numbers are bulky. A long string of 1's and 0's cannot be effectively transmitted from one individual to another; some shorthand method is necessary, and the octal number system fills this need. Because of its simple relationship to the binary system, numbers can be converted from one system to another by inspection.

The base or radix of the octal system is eight. There are no 8's or 9's in this number system. The important thing to remember is that three binary positions are equivalent to one octal position. Thus:

Binary System	Octal System
000	0
001	1
010	2
011	3
100	4
101	5
110	6
111	7

At this point a carry to the next-higher position of the number is necessary since all eight symbols have been used:

Binary System	Octal System
001 000	10
001 001	11
001 010	12
001 011	13
001 100	14

And so on.

The internal circuitry of the computer understands only binary 1's and 0's. However, the octal system is used to provide a shorthand method of reading and writing binary numbers, with the computer making the conversion.

Number Conversions

Before attempting to convert numbers from one system to another, it is best to review what a number represents. In the decimal system a number is represented or expressed by set values. Values are assigned to a power of ten and some integer from 0 to 9. For example, the number "123" means "100 plus 20 plus 3." This may also be expressed as

$$(1 \times 10^2) + (2 \times 10^1) + (3 \times 10^0).$$

Ten is said to be the base or radix of this system because of the role that the powers of ten and the integers up to ten play in this expansion. If two is chosen as the base, numbers are said to be represented in the binary system. Consider the binary number 1 111 011. The 0's and 1's represent the coefficients of the ascending power of two. Expressed in another way the number is

$$(1 \times 2^6) + (1 \times 2^5) + (1 \times 2^4) + (1 \times 2^3) + (1 \times 2^1) + (1 \times 2^0).$$

The various orders do not mean the same units, tens, hundreds, thousands, and the like as in the decimal system; instead, they signify units, twos, fours, eights, sixteens, and so on. The number "123" breaks down in both systems as follows:

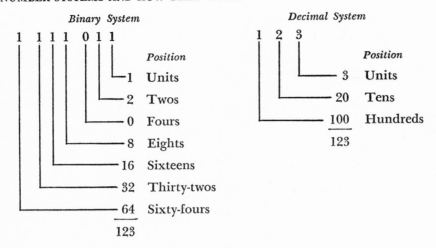

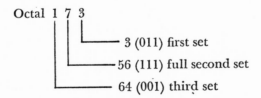

In the octal system, a number is represented in the same manner except that the base is eight. The digits of the number represent the coefficients of the ascending powers of eight. Consider the octal number:

$$173 = (1 \times 8^2) + (7 \times 8^1) + (3 \times 8^0)$$
$$= \quad 64 \quad + \quad 56 \quad + \quad 3$$
$$= \quad 123 \ (\text{decimal})$$

Similarly:

Octal 1 7 3
- 3 (011) first set
- 56 (111) full second set
- 64 (001) third set

By remembering what a number represents in the binary or octal system, it can be converted to its decimal equivalent as shown.

The Use of Integers

As numbers get bigger, however, this method becomes quite impossible. Other methods of converting from one system to another, here presented in detail, are needed.

Decimal to octal. To convert the decimal number "149" to its octal equivalent, the rule calls for dividing the decimal number by eight and developing the octal number as in the following example:

$$
\begin{array}{rl}
8 \mid & 149 \text{ Remainder } 5 \\
8 \mid & 18 \text{ Remainder } 2 \qquad = \quad 225 \\
8 \mid & 2 \text{ Remainder } 2 \\
& 0 \qquad\qquad\qquad \text{Read}
\end{array}
$$

We first divide the original number by 8. The remainder of this first division becomes the low-order digit of the conversion (5). We then divide the quotient (received from the first division) by 8, and again the remainder becomes a part of the answer (next-higher order, or 2). This process is continued until the quotient is smaller than the divisor. At this time the final quotient is considered the high order of the conversion (2).

Octal to decimal. The octal number 225, as an illustration, is converted to its decimal equivalent as follows:

$$
\begin{aligned}
225_{(8)} = 5 \times 8^0 = &5 \\
2 \times 8^1 = &16 \\
2 \times 8^2 = &128 \\
\hline
&149_{(10)}
\end{aligned}
$$

Octal to binary and binary to octal. The rule in this case is to express the number in binary groups of three:

Octal to Binary

2	2	5
010	010	101	= 010 010 101

Binary to Octal

010	010	101
2	2	5	= 225

Decimal to binary. Here the decimal number is divided by 2 and developed as in the example, where 149 is converted to its binary equivalent.

2		149	Remainder	1	
2		74	"	0	
2		37	"	1	
2		18	"	0	
2		9	"	1	= 010 010 101
2		4	"	0	
2		2	"	0	
2		1	"	1	
		0		Read	

BINARY TO DECIMAL

$$11101_{(2)} = 1 \times 2^0 = 1$$
$$0 \times 2^1 = 0$$
$$1 \times 2^2 = 4$$
$$1 \times 2^3 = 8$$
$$1 \times 2^4 = 16$$
$$\overline{29_{(10)}}$$

21. Putting a Job on the Computer

AFTER A PROBLEM HAS BEEN DEFINED BY SYSTEMS WRITE-UP, FLOW charts, and the like, five steps are required, in our example, to place a job on the computer. They are:
1. Prepare a block diagram.
2. Write the source program.
3. Assemble the source program into an object program.
4. Debug the object program.
5. Prepare documentation for the programing.

We shall assume a simple payroll problem defined as follows. Given (input):

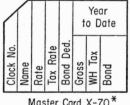

Master Card X-70*   Activity Card X-40

* X equals an identifying punch in a certain column to indicate what information is in the record.

To be developed (output):

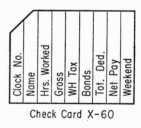

Check Card X-60   "No Master Card" X-50   Updated Master X-70

Using this problem, we shall go through the first three of our five steps.

A block diagram is a graphic representation of the operations and decisions involved in performing a given job. It need not be restricted to mechanical operations; it can apply as well to manual ones. For our purposes, the block diagram will pertain to the operations to be performed within the computer system.

In addition, there are usually card-handling operations external to the computer—punching, sorting, merging, selecting, reproducing, printing, and the like. A graphic description of this work is generally depicted on a flow chart. Exhibit 1 is a flow chart which describes the card handling external to the computer in our sample problem.

When the flow chart contains a computer function, as is the case in our problem, it is necessary that a block diagram be drawn to describe the computer processing. This may be done in two stages: first, a summary or general block diagram; second, a detailed block diagram. It is from the detailed diagram that the machine coding or programing will be done. Exhibit 2 shows a general block diagram which represents a transitional step from the computer function circled on the flow chart to the detailed block diagram shown in Exhibit 3. Note that only two different types of symbols are used in the block diagram as shown. The rectangular shape describes action, and the flattened oval indicates decisions. The number associated with each symbol is for the programer's convenience.

Suppose, at this time, we consider the following input cards and trace them through this diagram.

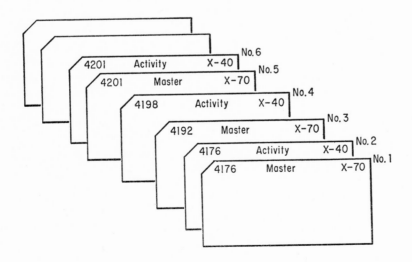

EXHIBIT 1
FLOW CHART

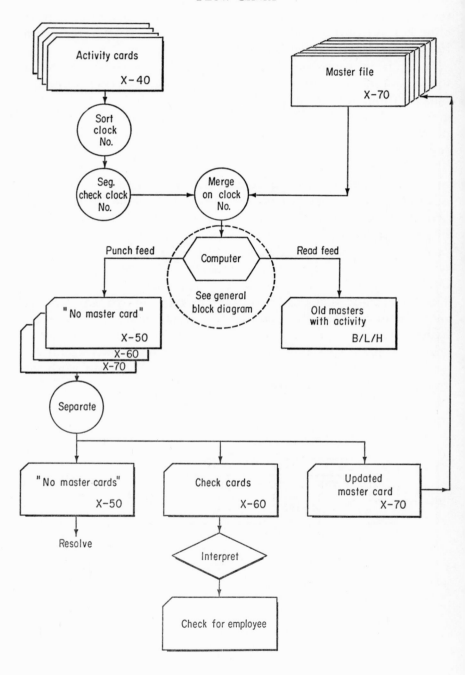

EXHIBIT 2
GENERAL BLOCK DIAGRAM

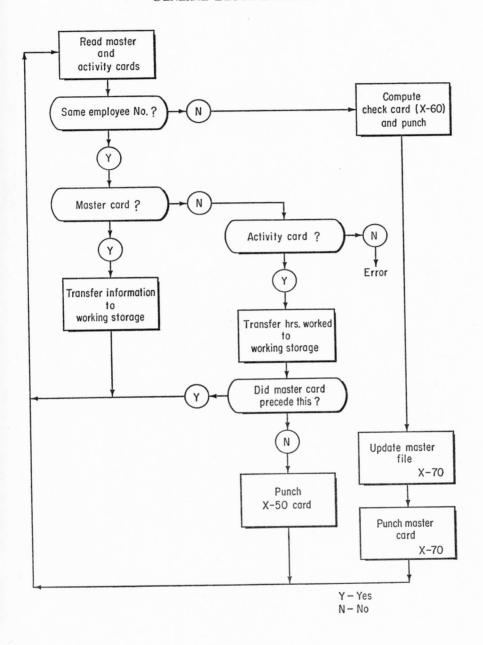

Y – Yes
N – No

EXHIBIT 3
DETAILED BLOCK DIAGRAM

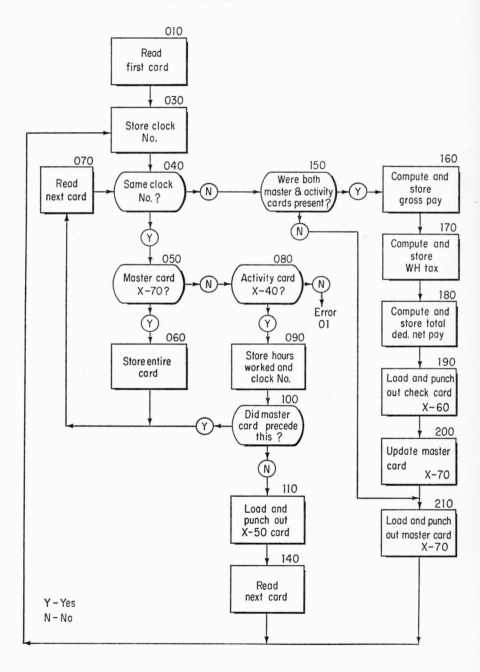

Y – Yes
N – No

The first symbol (labeled 010) provides for reading card 1 and recording an image of this card in a programer-assigned area in storage. This is often called the *read-in area*. Exhibit 4 shows the read-in area of storage and a detailed view of how card 1 appears in this area (for purposes of illustration, addresses 1951 through 1960 are used). Note that words consist of ten digits or five letters.

EXHIBIT 4
BLOWN-UP PICTURE OF STORAGE INPUT

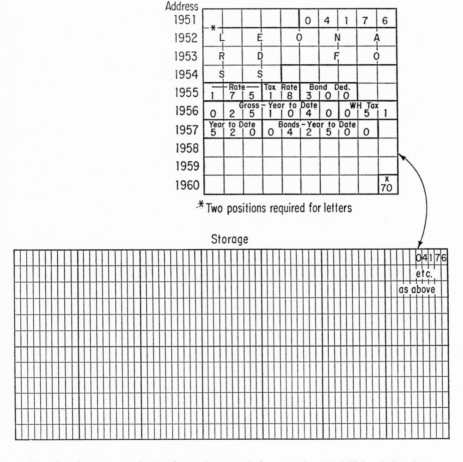

In the interest of clarity, the card image in Exhibit 4 is shown with data in the respective words; that is, 04176 in address 1951 is the clock number. Normally, we would not try to associate data with these words directly; rather, we would indicate the card columns to be assigned to the words. Exhibit 5 is the same card image repeated, but now we have indicated the card columns containing the data.

EXHIBIT 5

CARD COLUMNS ASSIGNED TO STORAGE POSITIONS

Address										
1951							1	2	CLOCK NO. 3	4	5
1952	6	6	7	7	NAME 8	8	9	9	10	10
1953	11	11	12	12	NAME 13	13	14	14	15	15
1954	16	16	17	17	NAME 18	18	19	19	20	20
1955	21	RATE 22	23	TAX RATE 24	25	BOND DED. 26	27	28		
1956	29	30	GROSS — YR. TO DATE 31	32	33	34	35	36	WH TAX 37	38
1957	YR. TO DATE 39	40	41	42	43	BONDS— YR. TO DATE 44	45	46	47	
1958										
1959										
1960										X 70

Decimal points are not punched in the card, hence do not appear in storage. Fields are planned on the card so that the decimal point is preplanned to fall between two columns; that is, in the rate field (Exhibit 5), the decimal point occurs between columns 21 and 22.

Starting now with the symbol labeled 030 (store clock number), we describe the action in storage for each step in the block diagram. (The prefix "S" in S030 can be interpreted as meaning "symbol.")

S030. The clock number from the read-in area must be recorded elsewhere in storage. (Because the next card to be read in will erase all previous information in the read-in area—addresses 1951 through

1960—it is necessary to transfer the data to be saved out of this area.) The question arises now as to where the clock number should be stored. Assuming the capacity of our storage is 2,000 words (with each word ten digits in length), we then see that we have a wide choice of available locations in which to place the clock number. Actually it is immaterial where we store it as long as we have the ability to recall it later as required. We could reserve some location—say, 0972—in which to store it, but if this is done the programer will need to remember the location so that when he needs the clock number later in the program he can refer to "0972."

A simpler method is available, however, in which we give the clock number a symbolic name and refer to it in storage by name rather than by a numeric, or absolute, address. In our example we shall store the information presently in address 1951 (clock number) in another location which we shall call CLOCK. This is symbolic coding designed for programing convenience; it will later be converted to absolute coding—that is, the name will be converted to an actual numeric or absolute address—by the computer. The action described in S030 will then cause storage to appear as shown in Exhibit 6.

EXHIBIT 6

Storage

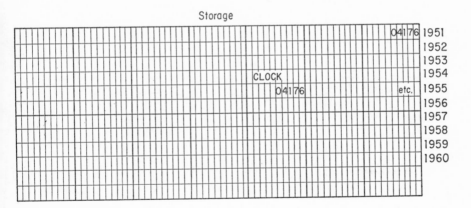

S040. This is a decision symbol, and the answer (yes or no) determines the path the program will follow. The clock number in address 1951 will be compared with the clock number in CLOCK; and, if it is the same (yes), the program will proceed to S050. Since we entered S040 from S030 (where we stored this same clock number), it becomes obvious that we are comparing a number with itself —in effect, forcing our path to go to S050. However, another entry into S040 (from S070) will record another card image in addresses 1951 through 1960, and this comparison may result in either a "yes" or a "no" answer to our question, "Is this the same clock number?" The meaning of action taken as a result of this comparison becomes more obvious when we reach card 2 and card 3 in our processing.

S050. By interrogating word 1960 the computer determines that this card (addresses 1951 through 1960) is an X-70 card, thereby directing the program to proceed to S060.

S060. The data now in addresses 1951 through 1960 will be transferred to another area in storage as shown in Exhibit 7. Data from 1951 have been transferred to "CLK70" (our symbolic notation meaning "clock number X-70 card"). Considerable freedom exists in the programer's choice of a symbolic address, but there are certain restrictions depending on the equipment used. To conform to the computer coding in our example, we can use one to five letters in our symbolic addresses, with numerals in lieu of the last two positions (as in CLK70) if desired.

Note that word 1955 (containing rate, tax rate, and bond deduction) is now stored in three different words: RATE, TAX RATE, and BOND. In short, each field has been "unpacked."

EXHIBIT 7

Storage

CLK70		04176	1951
NAMEA			1952
NAMEB			1953
NAMEC	CLOCK		1954
RATE	04176	etc.	1955
TRATE			1956
BOND			1957
YTDGR			1958
YTDWT	YTDBO		1959
			1960

Note: TRATE is tax rate; YTDGR, year-to-date gross; YTDWT, year-to-date withholding tax; and YTDBO, year-to-date bonds. These are known as mnemonic symbols.

Three words—NAMEA, NAMEB, and NAMEC (Names A, B, and C)—are used to store a name up to 15 letters and spaces in length. In the computer we are using for our example, two digits are required to represent a letter; hence the 15 letters and spaces in three ten-digit words (30 positions).

S070. At this point we read the next card—No. 2. The read-in area of memory will now appear as shown in Exhibit 8. From S070 the program proceeds to S040, where the clock number in address 1951 is compared with the clock number in CLOCK. In this case the answer is "yes"; so the program advances to S050. Interrogation of word 1960, however, reveals that this is not an X-70 card, and the program continues on to S080.

EXHIBIT 8

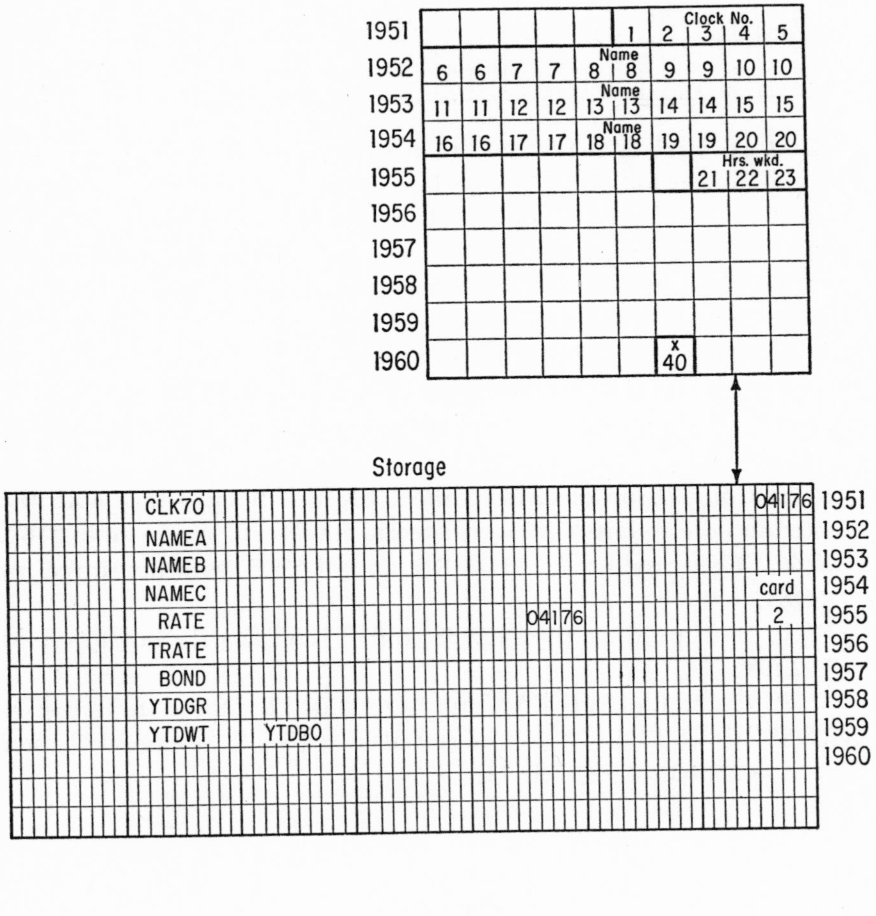

S080. Reference to word 1960 shows this to be an X-40 card.

S090. The clock number in address 1951 is stored in CLK40, and hours worked is stored in HOURS. (See Exhibit 9.)

EXHIBIT 9

Storage

	CLK70		CLK40			04176	1951
	NAME A		HOURS				1952
	NAME B						1953
	NAME C						1954
	RATE			04176			1955
	TRATE						1956
	BOND						1957
	YTDGR						1958
	YTDWT	YTDBO					1959
							1960

S100. A check is made now to see if the master card (X-70) and the activity card (X-40) information are for the same clock number. CLK70 and CLK40 are compared. If they are equal, we go to S070; if not, we go to S110. Since card 2 in our example is equal to the clock number stored in CLK70, the program will proceed to S070.

S070. S070 will bring another card image (No. 3) into the read-in area of storage. (See Exhibit 10.) S040 will compare the new clock number (04192) in address 1951 with the old clock number in CLOCK (04176). Since it is not the same, the program will advance to S150.

S150. Comparison of CLK70 and CLK40 will show that both the master and the activity card were present for 04176. We go on to S160.

S160. The product of HOURS and RATE will be stored in GROSS.

S170. The product of GROSS and TRATE will be stored in WHTAX.

S180. The sum of WHTAX and BOND will be stored in TODED; GROSS minus TODED will be stored in NETPA. Storage will then appear as shown in Exhibit 11.

EXHIBIT 10

Storage

	CLK70		CLK40			04 19 2	1951
	NAMEA		HOURS				1952
	NAMEB					card	1953
	NAMEC					3	1954
	RATE			04 17 6			1955
	TRATE						1956
	BOND						1957
	YTDGR						1958
	YTDWT	YTDBO					1959
							1960
						7 0	

EXHIBIT 11

Storage

	CLK70		CLK40			04 19 2	1951
	NAMEA		HOURS				1952
	NAMEB					card	1953
	NAMEC					3	1954
	RATE		GROSS	04 17 6			1955
	TRATE		WHTAX				1956
	BOND		TODED				1957
	YTDGR		NETPA				1958
	YTDWT	YTDBO					1959
							1960
							1961
						7 0	

S190. An area in storage must be reserved as output area in which a card image is created in the format desired for the card being punched. For our problem we shall designate words 1977 through 1986 as this area. Fields of information now scattered all over storage will be moved to this area and placed in such a way that the field arrangement desired on the check card (X-60) will be satisfied. Exhibit 12 shows storage as it appears after this action.

EXHIBIT 12

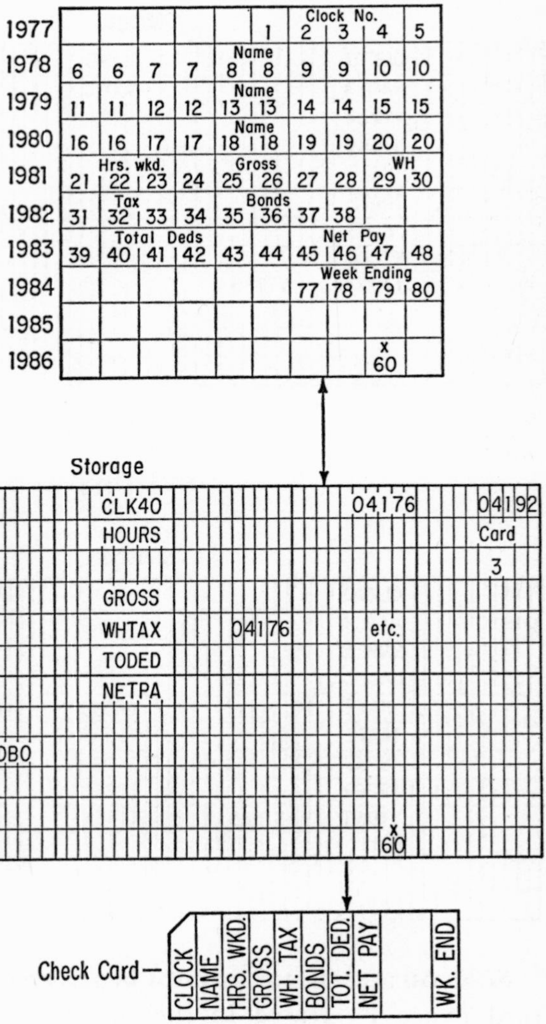

S200. The old **YTDGR** (year-to-date gross) will be increased by **GROSS** to give the new updated year-to-date gross pay. **WHTAX** will be added to YTDWT, and BOND will be added to YTDBO.

S210. The output area (addresses 1977 through 1986) will now be loaded from storage with the fields of information necessary to create a new updated X-70 master card. The format of this card will be the same as that of the input card shown in Exhibit 5.

S030 (it follows S210 on our block diagram) will result in the storage of 04192 in CLOCK. Recall that we now have card 3 in the read-in area (Exhibit 12) and that it will follow the block diagram through S040, S050, S060, and S070. The new card read in (No. 4) is an activity card for clock number 04198. S040 will then direct the program to S150, and a comparison between CLK70 (04192) and CLK40 (04176) will result in a "no" answer to the question asked in S150. As a result, the program branches to S210, where an X-70 card for clock number 04192 is created (in this case it will be a duplicate of the input card).

Continuing on to S030, we see that clock number (04198) in address 1951 will be stored in CLOCK. The path card (No. 4) will now trace in through S040, S050, S080, and S090. In S100, however, when a comparison is made between CLK70 (04192) and CLK40 (04198), the resulting answer will be "no" to the question asked by S100. The program will then advance to S110.

S110. Output area (addresses 1977 through 1986) will be loaded with the information for the S050 "no master card" so that it may be punched.

S140. This instruction will place an image of card 5 in the read-in area (addresses 1951 through 1960). The path traced by this card, beginning with S030, will be identical to that of card 1.

This description of the steps needed to computerize a payroll problem need not be fully understood. However, the reader should, by reviewing it even cursorily, be able to gain a general idea of the way in which a program is developed. This is really all that is necessary for our purposes. Those who wish to become programers will find there are special schools for their training. Technical matters are best left to them—the technicians.

*   *   *

Good documentation, so as to put a job in final shape for repetitive status, is a most impelling requirement for effective utilization of talent. It is possible, though impractical, for a technician to retain the details of an entire system in his memory for a time, and it is even possible to assign a man (or men) full-time to a system

EXHIBIT 13

Table of Contents for a Data Processing System

000.XX GENERAL
- .01 System Title Page
- .02 Table of Contents
- .03 Index
- .04 Change Control Log
- .05 Control Notices

100.XX SYSTEM
- .01 Purpose and Definition
- .02 Method—Processing Logic
- .03 Flow Chart—Program Through the System
- .04 Flow Chart—Data Through the System
- .05 Tape Control Sheets Exhibit

200.XX EAM AND KEYPUNCH INSTRUCTIONS
- .01 Incoming Documents—Definition and Handling
- .02 Keypunch Instructions
- .03 EAM Machine Flow
- .04 EAM Output—Control and Disposition

300.XX PROGRAM DOCUMENTATION (EDPM)
- .01 Purpose and Definition
- .02 Processing Logic
- .03 Restrictions
- .04 Flow Charts—General and Detail
- .05 Core Storage Assignment

400.XX EDPM CONTROL SECTIONS—INPUT HANDLING
- .01 Source and Medium
- .02 Input Card or Record Formats
- .03 Supporting Transmittals—Exhibits—Explanations

500.XX EDPM SETUP SECTIONS—FUNCTIONS
- .01 Prerequisites to Processing
- .02 Input—Medium
- .03 Run Sheet Exhibit
- .04 Label Exhibit
- .05 Operating Deck Format and Structure
- .06 Date, Rate, or Other "Special" Cards—Explanation

600.XX CPU OPERATING INSTRUCTIONS
- .01 On-Line Units Required
- .02 Loading Instructions
  - A. For Tape Units
  - B. For Card Read/Punch
  - C. For Printer—Includes Sample of Printout
- .03 Switch Settings
- .04 Special Action Required
- .05 Halts and Messages
- .06 Recovery Routines
- .07 Disposition of Input

700.XX BALANCING
- .01 Sample Control Form
- .02 Posting Instructions
- .03 Balancing Instructions

800.XX OUTPUT CONTROL
- .01 Medium
- .02 Disposition of Output
- .03 Tape Retention Schedule
- .04 Output Card, Record or Print Formats

900.XX SUPPORTING DOCUMENTATION
- .01 Assembly Listing
- .02 Patch Sheets

conceived and operated without formal documentation. This is, however, a most hazardous approach. Ill health, an accident, departure for a better job—all are constant threats to the successful operation of a system built on the quicksands of individual memory.

The time to document systems is before machine operations are designed, and the time for documenting corrections is before corrections are made. Therefore, when the first program is written, systems definition should be complete. When the last program is written and debugged (tested and corrected), documentation of all programing should be available. Exhibit 13 is a sample table of contents. The reader may not fully grasp all its detail, but he will nevertheless recognize it as a checklist of requirements for a well-documented data processing system.

When we consider that the cost of a system such as that outlined in Exhibit 13 may be upwards of $250,000 for design and programing, it seems only sane to insist on complete documentation to protect our investment. We would hardly build a facility without drawings or fail to insure it or to provide maintenance for it. Neither should we treat a costly data processing system so casually. The wise executive will insist on good documentation and control of change.

22. To Insure Reliable Output

ACCURACY IN ANY DATA PROCESSING SYSTEM IS NOT ACHIEVED without proper consideration and utilization of checks and controls. These checks may be divided into two broad areas: those built into the equipment and those written into the procedure by the systems man or by the programer.

Built-in Checks

Checks built into the equipment are designed as a safeguard against machine malfunction. When certain criteria are not satisfied in the operation of the equipment itself, a signal may be generated which will halt the program and indicate to the operator the nature of the malfunction. These checks, frequently referred to as *validity checks,* are of five types.

1. *Dual readings for comparison.* Two sets of read brushes are used in reading a card; if the two readings are not identical, the machine will stop. Magnetic tapes can have a "read after write" to determine whether what was read corresponds to what it was instructed to write. Also, some tapes have dual lanes on which the same information is recorded.

2. *Parity bit checks.* This term generally refers to data written on tape, magnetic or paper. A separate lane is reserved on which to record a magnetic spot (or punch) whenever the number of spots (vertical) for any given character is odd, thereby insuring that all characters read at a later time will consist of an even number of spots, including the parity bit. Failure to read an even number will result in machine detection of the error.

184

3. *Duplicate circuitry.* In some machines duplicate circuitry is provided for many operations. These are performed twice, one on each circuit, and the results are then compared for equality.

4. *Bit configuration checks.* If a machine is designed to use five bits (magnetic spots) to represent all digits, and any one digit requires two and only two bits, this constitutes a "2 out of 5" bit check.

5. *Timing and voltage checks.* Whenever voltage and certain time relationships are outside the designed operating range, the machine will stop.

Written-in Checks

Checks which can be written into the procedure or program are designed primarily as a safeguard against human errors. Some of these are:

1. *Record count.* The last record count, plus additions and minus deletions, equals the new record count. The last printed master list will contain a count of the records in the file. To this count must be added the additions to the file; then deletions or removals must be subtracted to give the new count.

2. *Control total.* This is a total of a field such as dollars or hours—or any other field where the unit of measure is the same.

3. *Hash total.* A hash total is made up of data that would ordinarily not be added into one sum, such as stock numbers, unit prices, and the like. It affords a control against the omission of entire records just as record counts do, but it has the additional advantage that a check is made to see that purely descriptive information has been read into the machine correctly.

4. *Limit check.* A field in a record or a result in a calculation may be checked to see whether certain predetermined limits have been exceeded. The limit check can be built into a payroll calculation program, for example, so that the amount of gross pay may not exceed a predetermined maximum—say, $200 per week.

5. *Crossfoot totals.* To continue our payroll example, gross minus tax minus bonds equals net.

6. *Double arithmetic.* $A + B = C$; $B + A = C$; $C = C$.

7. *Sequence check.* Each succeeding record in a file may be checked to see that it is in ascending sequence.

8. *Proof totals.* An important series of multiplications may be checked by a proof figure calculation. An arbitrary figure, which must be larger than any multiplier among the data to be verified, is selected as the proof figure. Each multiplicand is then multiplied twice, once by the multiplier originally provided in the data and a second time by the difference between the multiplier and the proof figure. The totals of both multiplications for all items processed are accumulated and compared with the product resulting from a multiplication of the total of all multiplicands by the proof figure. Thus:

Hours	Actual Rate	Proof Rate	Actual Extension	Proof Extension	
40	1.75	3.00	70.00	50.00	40(3.00 − 1.75)
38	2.20	3.00	83.60	30.40	38(3.00 − 2.20)
40	2.15	3.00	86.00	34.00	40(3.00 − 2.15)
118			239.60	114.40	

$118 \times 3.00 = 354.00 = 239.60 + 114.40.$

9. *Self-checking number (check digit).* There is a system of adding a check digit to identification numbers, such as part numbers or employee pay numbers, in accordance with a predetermined pattern. Errors in transcribing these numbers will then be detected by the machine during the processing. The use of self-checking numbers is not necessarily limited to electronic data processing installations.

A typical formula for self-checking numbers calls for multiplying the units position and every alternate digit of the desired identity number by two, adding the individual digits in the result and the digits not multiplied by two, and determining the number necessary to raise the resultant to the next higher multiple of ten. This number then becomes the final digit in the identity number. For example:

    a. Assume a part number of 62135.

    b. Multiply every other digit by 2, beginning at the left thus: $615 \times 2 = 1230.$

    c. The sum of new digits 1, 2, 3, and 0 plus old even digits 2 and 3 is 11.

    d. The number required to raise 11 to the next multiple of 10 (this is the check digit) is 9.

    e. The self-checking part number is 621359.

File Maintenance and Activity Processing

The processing of a file such as that for our sample payroll problem is supported as follows:

1. *File maintenance,* by which we mean adding to, deleting from, or changing the master file.

The master record file—one record per employee in our sample problem—contains data which are generally static or unchanging from pay period to pay period: name, clock number, hourly rate, and so on. When this file is initially set up, its contents must be clearly defined. For example, is it to have cards for all hourly employees or for all except those on the night shift? Then, once the file is set up, we must insure that no records will be lost, that additions, deletions, and changes will be properly made, and that back-up information will be available should it ever become necessary to reconstruct lost or damaged file records.

To satisfy these requirements, we must know the contents of the file when the job is begun; in other words, we must satisfy ourselves that the file does cover all hourly employees. If there are omissions, these must be accounted for at the time and recorded as exceptions so that the file listing is reconciled. This could be referred to as *completeness of file* or *file coverage.*

In the case of record changes, a count of the cards removed must equal a similar count when they are put back into the file. In the same way, the number of additions must be known before they are merged with the file and deletions likewise must be counted after removal. Knowing the number of records in last week's file, we arrive at the count for the new updated file by the formula

Old File + Additions − Deletions = New File.

A change may be considered to be both an addition and a deletion. When we have updated the new file, the count obtained must equal the count arrived at by the formula; and in the case of our payroll problem, as previously discussed, external controls need to be provided by an organization outside the data processing center.

2. *Activity processing*; that is, combining the periodic activity information with the master file information to provide the required

output. The activity cards in our sample problem consist of a new set of cards (one per employee) each pay period; on them we record the hours worked for this period. The supplier of the data should, in addition to the information itself, submit control counts or totals to the data processing center, which must set up internal controls to insure accuracy of processing.

In the event of wrong output, the processing center must be able to prove that all data supplied were properly processed. This proof can be supplied in the form of a transaction or record count, control totals, or hash totals. We might refer in this connection to *accountability of data*.

Application of Checks and Controls

In applying these controls we shall consider the entire job in three time phases, as follows:

1. *Preprocessing.* In this phase we shall be concerned with totals developed as a part of file maintenance (completeness of file) and activity processing (accountability of data). First let us consider file maintenance.

For our purpose we shall assume that our master file covers *all* hourly employees (file coverage) and is made up of the following cards:

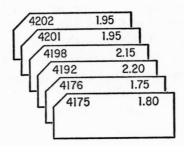

Although other information is included on the master cards, we have shown here only clock number and rate, since these are the fields that are of particular concern to us in controlling totals. A printed master list of the file would look like this:

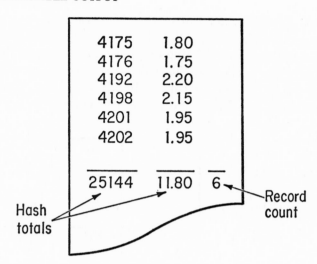

Adding the clock number and rate fields results in the two hash totals shown. A record count also is taken and recorded at the same time.

Suppose now that the master file needs to be updated to reflect additions (new hires) and deletions (terminations). Transmittals to the data processing center will provide information for these new hires and terminations as follows:

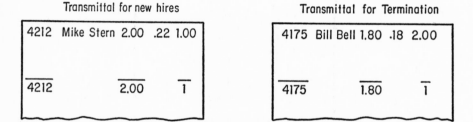

Cards will be punched from these transmittals as follows:

If volume is not great, deletions from the master file can be pulled manually; otherwise, cards will be punched as shown to serve as "search" cards for use in removing the desired records from the master file mechanically. Thus the example does not show rate on the search (pull) card; it will be on the card pulled. Here is the tabulation or printed list of the additions and deletions which will result:

Additions:

4212   2.00

——————————
4212   2.00   1

Deletions:

4175   1.80

——————————
4175   1.80   1

Then, after the card for clock 4212 has been merged into the master file and the card for clock 4175 has been removed, the file in its printed form will be altered accordingly. Thus:

4176   1.75
4192   2.20
4198   2.15
4201   1.95
4202   1.95
4212   2.00

——————————
25181   12.00   6

Application of the formula "Old File + Additions − Deletions = New File" should result in totals corresponding to those previously shown on the updated master list.

	Clock No.	Rate	Record Count
Old File	25144	11.80	6
Additions	4212	2.00	1
Deletions	4175−	1.80−	1−
	25181	12.00	6

Now for the activity processing side of phase 1. First, the weekly activity cards showing hours worked per employee will be punched from time cards or a transmittal as follows:

4175		T
4176	40.0	
4192	38.0	
4198	40.0	
4201	40.0	
4202	42.0	
4212	30.0	H
	230.0	7

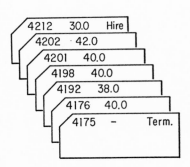

Although it is generally more desirable for the originator of data to develop control totals covering his transmittal, it sometimes is more convenient for these totals to be developed by machine (under controlled observation) within the data processing center immediately following their receipt. For this problem we shall assume that the summation of hours worked (230.0) was developed in the payroll department and a transmittal sent to data processing showing hours and record count. Here is the printed list of data from our cards:

4175	–	Term.
4176	40.0	
4192	38.0	
4198	40.0	
4201	40.0	
4202	42.0	
4212	30.0	Hire
	230.0	7

The control total (230.0) and record count (7) obtained from the punched cards correspond to the totals reported on the transmittal. Thus we have satisfied the accountability-of-data concept described previously.

2. *Processing.* When the job was programed, the following checks were built in: record count, control total, hash total, limit check, and crossfoot totals. During processing, the computer will count the number of records processed (6); sum up all clock numbers (25181); sum up hours worked (230.0); and arrive at rate (12.00), gross pay (459.50), WH tax deduction (85.12), bond deduction (15.50), total deductions (100.62), and net pay (358.88). In addition, the hours worked by each employee in excess of 60 (limit check) will be flagged for investigation before the payroll is released.

3. *Postprocessing.* Upon completion of machine processing, we can immediately determine validity through the use of control totals developed prior to processing and totals developed during processing. We begin with our accountability-of-output data:

	Preprocessing Totals	Processing Totals
Record count	6	6
Hash totals: clock no.	25181	25181
rate	1200	1200
Control totals: hours	230	230
deductions, bond	1550	1550
deductions, WH tax	——	8512

Crossfoot	——	
	459.50	(gross)
	−15.50	(bond ded.)
	−85.12	(WH tax)
	= 358.88	(net pay)

Proof by rate category:

Hours	Rate		
40.0	1.75	=	70.00
82.0	1.95	=	159.90
30.0	2.00	=	60.00
40.0	2.15	=	86.00
38.0	2.20	=	83.60
230.0			$459.50

In developing proof by rate category, a location in memory could be assigned to each respective rate in which would be summed up the total number of hours worked during the week at that given rate. For example: Clock numbers 4201 and 4202 both have an hourly rate of $1.95. The sum of the hours worked for these two employees is 82.0 hours. When machine processing is finished, the extensions for each rate can be made automatically by the computer to develop a sum representing the gross pay (459.50 in this example).

These same extensions can be performed manually on a Comptometer with a minimum of effort to provide an additional check. Calculated deductions, such as withholding tax, FICA, retirement, and the like, can be proved in a similar manner.

Provision for reconstruction of data must be made. In the event of a machine malfunction or human error, much information could be garbled or even lost. However, the proper use of preprocessing and processing checks should detect the difficulty. In our example, reference to last week's master list (proved correct at that time) and lists of this week's change activity will enable us to reconstruct the files.

Here follows the three-generation philosophy of data retention applied to magnetic tape files.

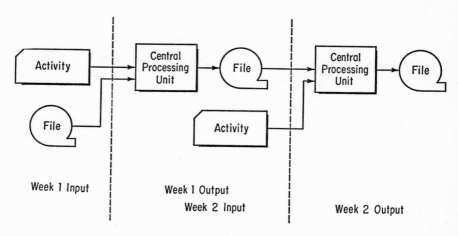

If, while processing week 2, the input file is found to be faulty or becomes damaged, the tape file and the activity cards shown in the input for week 1 can be used to reconstruct the file before continuing on with week 2.

Glossary

Glossary of Terms Often Used
In Data Processing and Computing

access time—time required in a computer to move information from memory to compute mechanism.

accumulator—the unit where numbers are totaled (accumulated).

address—a location, either name or number, where information may be stored.

add-subtract time—time required to add or subtract, not including access time. Sometimes referred to as **internal speed.**

ADP—automatic data processing.

alphabetic-numeric—pertaining to letters of the alphabet and numerals.

analog computer—a computer in which numbers are represented by physical magnitudes such as the amount of rotation of a shaft or a quantity of electrical voltage or current. Nomographs or charts which represent quantities of lengths of lines on a sheet of paper are of the analog type. See also **digital computer.**

arithmetic operations—addition, subtraction, multiplication, and division.

arithmetic unit—place where arithmetic operations are performed, as opposed to storage.

auxiliary storage—storage outside the computer, as on drums or random or direct access discs.

available machine time—time when machine is turned on and in good working order, not including maintenance time.

binary. See **binary number system.**

binary coded decimal—a system of representing decimal numbers in which each decimal digit is composed of one or more of four binary bits.

binary to decimal conversion—converting from binary to decimal system, as from 1111 to 15.

binary digit, bit—general name for either of the symbols ("on" or "off") in the binary system. See also **bit binary.**

binary number system—a number system using the base two. There are only two symbols: one (on) and zero (off). Digit values reading from right to left are: 1, 2, 4, 8, 16, 32, etc.

bit binary—smallest unit of information in the binary system. A bit binary is 1 or 0, more commonly called "yes" or "no," "on" or "off," etc., to describe the condition of the magnetic core or other recording device. The decimal number 15 is 1111 in the binary system; that is, these four bits are in a "yes" or "on" condition.

block diagram—a chart showing the flow of operations through a computer.

block of information—a group of numbers or "words."

block sort—the technique of breaking large quantities of detail into smaller groups for sorting on EAM equipment. This is accomplished by sorting first on a high-order digit and then making later sorts by groups.

bootstrap instructions. See **self-loading.**

branch, branch point—the start of two possible sequences of instructions only one of which is logically selected to be executed. The choice of paths is made by the machine according to a predetermined instruction, depending on whether some number is positive or negative, zero or nonzero. The ability to make this simple choice is the source of the application by some people of the term "brain" to the machine.

break point—a point in a routine at which the computer may, under the control of a manually set switch, be stopped for an operator's check on the progress of the routine.

buffer—a storage unit in which information is accumulated and held for later use; a bucket for putting away information to be poured out later. Sometimes called **buffer storage.** Generally used to balance two or more devices of varying speeds.

built-in check—a device or method for double-checking the computer's accuracy.

call-in—the act of instructing the computer to bring in information or instructions.

capacity—what the computer will hold; quantity of data it will store and use at any one time. Usually applied in describing storage.

card column—a column of information where single digits or alphabetic characters may be put (EAM) or where binary information may be punched (EDPM), giving values to numbers relating to binary digits.

card field—a group of card columns usually assigned for a specific use just as a worksheet in manual clerical operations may have a group of columns for a designated purpose. For example, six card columns (a field) will allow the recording of a six-digit invoice number.

card master—a file which is used for storing established facts such as employee rate, number, name, date of birth, and date of hire.

card-programed computer—a computer which may be instructed by a card program deck (cards arranged logically in sequence). Tape may be used on some machines, both cards and tapes on others.

card punch—a machine designed to punch holes in cards and controlled to punch in specified columns as desired. May be operated manually or automatically from other cards. May be prepared by computers or EAM equipment equipped with a card punch attached.

card reader—a device designed to read the holes punched in cards and to use this information to perform another function such as reading into a computer, punching other cards, making magnetic tape recordings, or printing.

cathode ray tube—a vacuum tube, similar to a television picture tube, used for displaying information. Also called **electrostatic storage tube.**

channel—the route of data flow; the path through which information passes.

character—a number or letter or other meaningful symbol.

character printer. See **printer.**

check bit—a character whose absence or presence, when compared to its accompanying letter or number symbols, will indicate proper content of the letter or number. Also called **parity check.**

check point (CP)—a reference point at which error-free operation of the program has been verified and to which the program may return for restart in the event of subsequent failure. Also refers to that routine in the program which writes the check-point record.

code—(1) a group of symbols used to classify a thing or person. Example: Code 1, single man; code 2, married man; etc. (2) To use symbols to instruct machines.

collate—to combine two files into one in a desired sequence; the machine action which automatically combines two or more groups of data.

collating sequence—the relative order of precedence assigned to numbers, letters, and special characters.

command—an instruction.

common language—a language which may be used by two or more machines without alteration or change.

compiler—a routine designed to produce a desired program automatically.

computer—an electronic data processing machine capable of receiving external instruction to perform a set of logical acts internally.

conditional transfer—usually a transfer of control, which will take place only if a certain condition is satisfied.

console—the control panel of a computer where the machine's actions may be observed and controlled.

control, control field—(1) designated card columns, or magnetic characters in a tape, representing a desired grouping for information display or totaling. Example: Card columns 1 through 3 are used to designate department number; when all cards have been run through for employees in department 001, the control on the department will cause a total to be printed. (2) The act of controlling on such fields.

control word (CW)—that part of a record made up of selected characters or fields of characters upon which the record is sorted. Also sometimes referred to as the **key.**

conversion—the changing of a number representation from one number system to another; for example, changing decimal numbers to binary numbers.

core—a name commonly used in describing the doughnut-shaped magnets which, in prearranged and meaningful groups, comprise "the core." Magnets are energized (on) or in a normal state (off) and are checked for condition by "sense" circuits. See also **bit binary.**

counter—a device for counting symbolic impulses or numbers.

crystal rectifier. See **diode.**

cycle—a machine cycle; the complete cycle of a machine.

cycle time—the time taken for the machine to go through a set of operations.

data collection—the act of gathering and recording data mechanically at the originating point.

data processing machine—in general, a machine which can store and process numeric and alphabetic information. See also **analog computer** and **digital computer.**

data reduction—arranging information in a manner which will make it meaningful and useful.

data transmission—the communication of data, usually over long distances by wire or microwave. Generally differs from data collection in that information has already been gathered, or collected, before it is transmitted.

decimal to binary—relating to the conversion of a number expressed in decimal language to binary language. Example: 15 equals 1111.

decimal number system—the common number system using the base ten, the symbols for which are 0, 1, 2, 3, 4, 5, 6, 7, 8, 9. Column unit values, reading from right to left, are 1, 10, 100, 1000, etc.

digit—a numeral from zero to nine in the decimal system.

digital computer—a machine which works with a system of mathematics having specified values.

diode—an electrical element, used in computing machine construction, which will pass current in one direction only. Also called **crystal diode, crystal rectifier, germanium diode.**

direct access. See **random access.**

disc. See **magnetic disc.**

drum. See **magnetic drum.**

EAM—punched card equipment (electric accounting machine).

edit—(1) machine action to establish propriety or need for data; (2) to take such action.

EDPM. See **computer.**

electrostatic storage tube. See **cathode ray tube.**

encoding—generally, using input in one language to produce output in another language.

erase—remove data from magnetic tape or other record.

exit—a place for removal of internal information (EAM) or a way of testing for stopping a routine by sampling totals, etc.

feedback—a return of information for use or alteration.

field length—the length of a field or grouping of digits on punched cards. See also **record length.**

file maintenance—the maintenance of a data processing file; updating of a file.

fixed-length records—records comprising a file in which every record is the same length.

fixed-point system—a system of handling numbers in which the point separating fractions from whole numbers is always situated between the same columns.

flip-flop—a descriptive term used generally to describe the "on-off" principle of electronic storage devices.

flip-flop storage. See **vacuum tube storage.**

floating-point system—a system of handling numbers in which each number has a fixed point and an associated multiplier. The multiplier serves to reduce the number of zeros needed to represent the desired value. This applies to decimal, binary, and other number systems. See also **fixed-point system.**

flow chart—(1) in computing, the flow of information through a computer programing plan; (2) graphic description of information flow.

gangpunch—to punch the same information in more than one card. Example: Gangpunch week-ending data in all time cards.

germanium diode. See **diode.**

grouping (G)—the number of records ordered in memory by the internal sort. Also called **records internally sorted (RIS).**

hash total—a total of designated numbers (such as employee numbers), used as a checking device, which has no significance except as a balancing medium to see if all records are present.

IDP—integrated data processing. The term is loosely used to describe the marrying of related groups of machines or systems.

illegal characters—bit combinations which are not acceptable to the computer or to a given program.

indexing—usually, a method of address modification.

initialization—resetting counters, switches, and instruction addresses at specified points in a program. Not to be confused with the assignment program which is performed only once and is always executed before the running program has been started.

input—information going into a system or instructions to a computer.

instruction—a command to the machine (in a program) to do something.

integrated data processing. See **IDP.**

internal speed. See **add-subtract time.**

interpreter, EAM—a machine which prints on the card the information that is punched therein.

interpreter, computer—a routine for interpreting information accumulated or computed in a routine or program.

internal sort—a process whereby several records are stored in a memory while their proper order is established according to their control words.

internal storage—storage which is an integral part of the machine, as opposed to magnetic drums or peripheral devices.

jack panel—a plugboard.

key—a term synonymous with "control word." Also sometimes used to describe a set of memory addresses which refer to the location of records.

keypunch—a manually operated machine for punching holes in cards.

key verify—a repetitive operation (except that no punching is performed) to insure punching was correct, performed on a **key verifier.**

language. See **common language.**

line printer. See **printer.**

logic—the reasoning processes applied to machines as well as people.

logical operations—those basic operations of the machine which are not arithmetic and not part of input or output. See also **conditional transfer.**

loop—a series of instructions, the last of which directs the machine to start again at the first of the series.

machine cycle. See **cycle.**

machine language. See **common language.**

magnetic disc—a disc resembling a phonograph record coated with ferrous material and marked with designated channels and "spots." It spins at a high rate of speed and is "sensed" by a movable arm set on instruction (command).

magnetic drum—a rotating cylinder surfaced with a material which can be magnetized. Information is stored on the drum by the presence or absence of magnetized spots in prescribed patterns.

mark sensing—a manual operation that consists of marking numerals on cards in designated "spots" with a soft (graphite) pencil. A machine "reads" such pencil marks and punches the numerals in card columns as desired.

memory, memory device. See **core** and **storage.**

merge—to put together two or more files by collating, etc.

microsecond—one-millionth of a second.

millisecond—one-thousandth of a second.

module—an interchangeable unit; a plug-in unit to replace or expand.

monitor—to watch the computer by means of the "console" or a programed routine.

multiple-address instruction—a program system which can specify the location of more than one number in a memory; the operation to be performed on these numbers; the location in which the result of the operation on these numbers should be stored; and, in some cases, the address of the next instruction.

nanosecond—one-billionth of a second.

on line—operating in conjunction with main equipment.

on-line printing—printing information directly from the computer during a job.

open subroutine—a subroutine inserted directly into a linear sequence of instructions, not entered by reference. Such a subroutine must be recopied at each point that it is needed in a routine.

operation—a specific action which the machine will automatically perform whenever an instruction calls for it (addition, transfer zero test, etc.).

order. See **instruction.**

order of merge—the number of files which can be combined into a consolidated file during a merging operation or during the merging phase of a sort.

output—a production of the computer or EAM routine or system; a report, a tape, cards, etc.

output device—part of a machine which translates the intangible electrical impulses processed by the machine into tangible permanent results: printed forms, punched cards, or magnetic "writing" on magnetic tape.

panel control—(1) a wiring board, "jack board," external wiring for instruction of the machine; (2) a display unit to show the action of the machine.

parallel operation—an operation within the arithmetic section of a machine such that all digits of a number are handled simultaneously. For example, the usual desk adding machine has a parallel type of operation.

parity check. See **check bit.**

pass—a complete cycle of reading, processing, and output on a program.

permanent storage—the medium used to retain intermediate or final results outside the machine, usually in the form of punched cards, punched paper tape, or magnetic tape. See also **output device.**

picosecond—one-trillionth of a second.

preventive maintenance—maintenance performed, when nothing is malfunctioning, to avoid future malfunction.

printer—a unit of the machine which prints characters from cards or tape or directly from the computer. Numbers, letters, or symbols may be printed, depending on the device. Also called **line printer, character printer.**

program—(1) to instruct the computer; (2) a series of commands to the computer.

programer—one who programs.

programing step—usually one instruction in a program.

program counter—the device in the control unit of the machine which is used for the selection of program steps or instructions in a simple sequence.

program tape—a magnetic tape on which the program is recorded.

pulse—an electrical current or voltage which exists only for a brief period of time.

punched card—a card in which holes are punched and which may be "read" by computers or EAM equipment. Punched card machines usually operate from punched cards only.

random access—the ability to go directly to desired information without passing through other information. See **magnetic disc** for an example of random access equipment. Also called **direct access.**

read, read in, read out—the operation of transferring information from one location to another. For example, paper tape, punched cards, or magnetic tape may be read and the information they contain may be transferred to other storage locations within a machine.

real time—term used to refer to the solution of problems relating to a set of conditions while the conditions are being generated. Example: Checking the flight of a missile while it is in flight.

record count—the number of items or records in a file.

record length—the length of a field or grouping of digits on magnetic tape. See also **field length.**

records internally sorted (RIS). See **grouping.**

reel—a spool on which tape is kept.

register—another name for a particular storage location, usually in the arithmetic section of a machine.

reproducer—an EAM machine which can reproduce information from one file into another or which can produce a file from information in another. See also **gangpunch.**

reset—to return to normal.

routine—a sequence of operations.

secondary storage—storage not an integral part of the computer. See also **auxiliary storage.**

self-loading—a sequence of instructions which are so constructed that the first few make the machine automatically accept and store those that follow. Sometimes referred to as a bootstrap operation, since it literally lifts itself into the machine.

sequence—a string or group of items in either ascending or descending order. Ascending order is implied unless descending is specified. The length of each sequence can be one or more records.

sequence break—a condition that exists when a record has a lower-valued control word (in the collating sequence) than the preceding record. The preceding sequence is concluded and a new one must be started. When sorting in reverse order, a sequence break is just the reverse: In this case, sequence break or "step down" is the condition which arises when the control word of a new record has a higher value than the control word of the preceding record.

sequence check—an operation to see that data are in the desired order.

serial operation—the type of operation within the arithmetic section of a machine such that a number is handled one digit at a time. See also **parallel operation.**

sign, sign digit—the symbol or symbols which distinguish positive (+) from negative (−) numbers for a machine.

significant digits—meaningful digits in coding. Example: If 1X means sheets and X3 means green, 13 will designate green sheets.

simulation—generally, the process of making one piece of equipment operate as another; to emulate an old machine, thus avoiding reprograming.

single-address instruction—an instruction which usually contains one operation and the address (location) of one number on which the operation is to be performed. See also **multiple-address instruction.**

sort—to place a file of records in order according to designated control word data.

sorter, EAM—a machine designed to arrange cards in sequence. See also **block sort.**

step down. See **sequence break.**

storage—the unit used to store information. See also **core.**

storage surface. See **cathode ray tube, magnetic drum, magnetic tape.**

store—to use storage for holding information.

stored program—a characteristic of certain machines such that instructions in the form of numbers, letters, or symbols are held within the machine. The machine refers to these instructions in a specified sequence and performs the operations specified by the instructions.

subroutine—a routine called out as desired but not necessarily written in the main program.

summary punch—a machine for punching cards on output of EAM equipment.

symbolic coding—a system of coding which uses symbols instead of addresses; a tool for simplifying programing.

tabulating equipment. See **EAM.**

tabulator. See **printer.**

tape—magnetic or punched paper tape.

tape feed—a device for "passing" tape.

tape label—a record, usually at the beginning or end of the tape, or both, designated for purposes of identification and control. Tape labels have many
functions: to identify the input records as belonging to the desired file;
to confirm that the tape reels put on tape units for output may be used as
output tapes; to contain the purge data; to check the switch settings and
manual operations of the console operator, etc. Labels at the end of a
tape usually contain record count, control totals, and end-of-job notations.

temporary storage. See **storage.**

test routine—a routine to test the machine for proper operation.

three-address instruction—an instruction which contains three addresses and
one operation. A machine will call two numbers from the first two addresses
(locations), perform the required operation, and store the result in the
third address.

transfer—(1) transfer of control, or transfer instruction, which causes the
machine to change its normal sequence of operations; (2) transfer of data—
that is, the moving of a number from one storage location to another. See
also **conditional transfer.**

update. See **file maintenance.**

vacuum tube storage—vacuum tubes and their associated electrical circuits,
sometimes used to store information in older machines.

variable length records—records comprising a file in which the number of
characters in each record varies.

verifier. See **key verifier.**

word—usually a fixed number of characters in a computer. For example, ten
characters may be called a "word."

write—the operation of storing a number on the surface of a magnetic tape,
magnetic drum, or cathode ray tube.

zero suppression—the elimination of nonsignificant zeros to the left of the
integral part of a quantity before printing is begun.

About the Author

Paul T. Smith is assistant controller for General Dynamics Corporation in Fort Worth, Texas. He attended Texas Wesleyan College.

Mr. Smith's experience in data processing spans a quarter of a century—as a machine operator, as data processing department head, and in executive positions responsible for directing large data processing programs. He served as manager of systems, North American Aviation, Inc., and as controller of Temco Aircraft Corporation (now Ling Temco Vought) before joining General Dynamics. His experience includes application of mechanized systems to commercial ventures as well as to the defense industry, and he is well known in industry for system-oriented controllership.